Inglês
básico nas organizações

Inglês
básico nas organizações

Thereza Cristina de Souza Lima
Carmen Terezinha Koppe

Av. Vicente Machado, nº 317 · 14º andar
Centro · CEP 80420-010 · Curitiba · PR · Brasil
Fone: [41] 2103-7306
www.editoraintersaberes.com.br
editora@editoraintersaberes.com.br

Conselho editorial Dr. Ivo José Both (presidente), Drª Elena Godoy, Dr. Nelson Luís Dias, Dr. Ulf Gregor Baranow
Editor-chefe Lindsay Azambuja
Editor-assistente Ariadne Nunes Wenger
Editor de arte Raphael Bernadelli

Preparação de originais Priscilla Cesar
Projeto gráfico e diagramação Sílvio Gabriel Spannenberg
Capa Roberto Querido
Ilustrações André Figueiredo Muller
Iconografia Sandra Sebastião

Dados Internacionais de Catalogação na Publicação (CIP)
(Câmara Brasileira do Livro, SP, Brasil)

Lima, Thereza Cristina de Souza
   Inglês básico nas organizações / Thereza Cristina de Souza Lima, Carmen Terezinha Koppe. – Curitiba: InterSaberes, 2013.

   Bibliografia
   ISBN 978-85-8212-158-0

   1. Administração 2. Inglês – Estudo e ensino I. Koppe, Carmen Terezinha. II. Título.

13-01532   CDD-420.7

Índices para catálogo sistemático:
1. Inglês: Áreas de administração: Estudo e ensino   420.7

1ª edição, 2013.
Foi feito o depósito legal.

Informamos que é de inteira responsabilidade das autoras a emissão de conceitos.

Nenhuma parte desta publicação poderá ser reproduzida por qualquer meio ou forma sem a prévia autorização da Editora InterSaberes.

A violação dos direitos autorais é crime estabelecido na Lei nº 9.610/1998 e punido pelo art. 184 do Código Penal.

Sumário

Prefácio **9**

Apresentação **11**

Capítulo 1
Apresentação do idioma inglês e sua importância na comunicação empresarial 13
Conceituação de inglês instrumental (*English for Specific Purposes* – ESP) **13**
Primeiro passo para leitura e compreensão de textos **14**
Semelhança entre as línguas e ordem dos vocábulos nas sentenças **15**
Conceituação de *cognato*, *skimming* e *scanning* **15**
Como lemos? **16**
Five strategies for good readers **17**
Verbos **18**
Advérbios **21**
Short answers **24**
Greetings (cumprimentos) **24**
Exercise Approaching Collocations **27**
Síntese do capítulo **27**

Capítulo 2
Organizar e administrar o tempo 29
Agenda **29**
WH questions **30**
Numbers **33**
Datas **34**
What time is it? What's the time? **35**
Present Continuous/Present Progressive **36**
How to choose your profession **37**
Pronomes demonstrativos **39**
Simple Present × Present Continuous (Progressive) **39**
Exercise Approaching Collocations **43**
Síntese do capítulo **44**

Capítulo 3
Qualidade de vida no ambiente de trabalho 45
Writing informal letters **46**
The Simple Past **48**
Possessive adjectives **50**
Prefixos e sufixos **53**
Verbo *to be*: in the past **58**
Business meetings **59**
Exercises Approaching Collocations **60**
Síntese do capítulo **61**

Capítulo 4
Meios de transporte 63
Pronomes interrogativos iniciados com *how* **65**
Substantivos e advérbios contáveis e incontáveis **67**
Reflexive pronouns **70**
Plural **71**
Exercise Approaching Collocations **73**
Síntese do capítulo **73**

Capítulo 5
Vestuário adequado para o ambiente de trabalho 75
Work dress codes and image collection **75**
How to dress to impress on Casual Fridays **76**
Futuro **77**
Negotiating **80**
Comparisons **81**
Grau dos adjetivos **82**
Exercise Approaching Collocations **86**
Síntese do capítulo **86**

Capítulo 6
Refeições na empresa 87
Modal verbs **89**
Preposições **92**
Etiquette tips for the business dinner **98**
Exercises Approaching Collocations **100**
Síntese do capítulo **101**

Capítulo 7
O escritório/The office 103
Present Perfect 104
Usando *for* e *since* 106
Tips on answering the phone at work 107
Exercise Approaching Collocations 110
Síntese do capítulo 111

Capítulo 8
Viagens de negócios 113
Business Trip 113
Used to e o uso do infinitivo e do gerúndio 114
Uso de *too*, *enough*, *so* e *such* 116
Organizing business trips 117
Other important information 118
Exercise Approaching Collocations 119
Síntese do capítulo 120

Capítulo 9
O hotel/The hotel 121
Writing an e-mail 121
Relative pronouns 122
Past Perfect, the use of yet, just and already 125
The pronouns where, when, why 127
Exercise Approaching Collocations 128
Síntese do capítulo 128

Capítulo 10
Reuniões, conferências e palestras 129
Writing a report 129
Passive voice (Voz passiva) 131
Conectivos (*connectives*) 134
Dificuldades especiais 138
Exercises Approaching Collocations 138
Síntese do capítulo 139

Capítulo 11
Apresentando-se em uma entrevista **141**
Having a job interview **141**
Discurso direto e indireto **142**
Writing a Curriculum Vitae (CV) **146**
Exercise Approaching Collocations **148**
Síntese do capítulo **149**

Capítulo 12
Correspondência empresarial **151**
Writing formal letters **151**
Phrasal verbs **154**
Dificuldades especiais **155**
Idiomatic expressions **157**
Exercise Approaching Collocations **158**
Síntese do capítulo **158**

Considerações finais **159**

Glossário **161**

Referências **167**

Apêndices **171]**
Apêndice 1: Verbos irregulares **171**
Apêndice 2: Falsos cognatos **176**
Apêndice 3: Idioms **181**
Apêndice 4: Phrasal verbs **183**

Chave de respostas **185**

Sobre as autoras **205**

Prefácio

O fim do século XX e o início do século XXI têm sido marcados por mudanças importantes, principalmente na área profissional, em decorrência do advento do computador, que possibilitou a comunicação rápida e efetiva entre empresas nacionais e multinacionais. Com essa interação, o domínio de uma língua estrangeira – mais especificamente, a inglesa – tornou-se indispensável, especialmente para o profissional voltado aos negócios.

O estudante orientado para o mundo empresarial deve levar em conta essas mudanças e aprimorar de maneira crescente seus conhecimentos de língua inglesa. É isso que este livro propicia, em uma abordagem clara e concisa, utilizando, sobretudo, um vocabulário abrangente, direcionado àqueles que necessitam desenvolver atividades em inglês.

A presente obra vem ao encontro dessa necessidade, ao possibilitar uma aprendizagem mais ampla e prática da língua inglesa, abordando tanto aspectos sintáticos e semânticos como o desenvolvimento da compreensão de textos. Os aspectos sintáticos são explicados de forma simples e precisa, mantendo-se sempre a preocupação com a exemplificação e com a aplicação dos conceitos, tornando prazeroso o trabalho com diferentes gêneros textuais e fazendo com que o potencial do profissional seja plenamente aproveitado. Este livro facilita, pois, a aquisição dos conhecimentos, acelera o processo de aprendizagem e oferece maiores condições para o uso da língua inglesa por parte de alunos envolvidos em diversos ambientes profissionais.

Drª Diva Cardoso de Camargo

Apresentação

Atualmente, o inglês está presente em todo tipo de comunicação, seja escrita, seja oral. Assim, a maioria dos cursos universitários exige, no mínimo, o domínio básico dessa língua. Com o propósito de possibilitar esse conhecimento, buscamos despertar nos leitores o prazer em desenvolver uma relação mais abrangente com o inglês.

Para alcançarmos esse objetivo – ou seja, para que os caminhos de aprendizagem da língua inglesa se tornem prazerosos –, iniciamos todos os capítulos com um texto referente a algum tópico relevante para o estudante e o (futuro) profissional, trabalhando com gêneros textuais diversos. A sintaxe e a semântica são abordadas com vistas à compreensão dos textos apresentados.

Esperamos que, ao longo dos temas abordados, possamos contribuir de maneira positiva para o aprendizado de cada um dos leitores desta obra.

Assim, este livro está dividido em 12 capítulos e cada um deles aborda um ou mais assuntos referentes à organização sintática da língua inglesa, além trazer textos diversos para leitura, explicações, exemplos, exercícios e curiosidades para que o processo de aprendizagem se torne algo motivante. Esta obra apresenta, também, um glossário organizado por capítulos, para facilitar a busca do significado das palavras.

Desejamos que as expectativas dos leitores sejam atendidas de maneira satisfatória e que esta obra seja importante em sua vida profissional.

Temas

Em cada capítulo, exploramos um tema diferente, sempre relacionado ao gênero textual abordado.

- Capítulo 1 – Estratégias de leitura
- Capítulo 2 – Boa utilização do tempo
- Capítulo 3 – Qualidade de vida no ambiente de trabalho
- Capítulo 4 – Meios de transporte
- Capítulo 5 – Vestuário adequado para o ambiente de trabalho
- Capítulo 6 – Refeições na empresa
- Capítulo 7 – Telefonemas de negócios
- Capítulo 8 – Viagens de negócios
- Capítulo 9 – Reservas de hotel
- Capítulo 10 – Reuniões, conferências e palestras
- Capítulo 11 – *Curriculum vitae*
- Capítulo 12 – Correspondência empresarial

Apresentação do idioma inglês e sua importância na comunicação empresarial

Muitas pessoas ouvem a expressão *língua franca* e não sabem do que se trata. Procter (1995, p. 827, tradução livre das autoras) define tal expressão como "a língua que é usada para a comunicação entre grupos de pessoas que falam idiomas diferentes, mas que não é usada entre os membros de um mesmo grupo"[1]. Assim como o latim foi a língua franca do Império Romano, atualmente se considera o inglês a língua franca do mundo globalizado. Por consequência, o conhecimento desse idioma tornou-se um pré-requisito imprescindível na maioria das áreas, sobretudo na empresarial.

Este livro tem como objetivo principal habilitar o estudante voltado para o mundo empresarial a se comunicar por meio da língua inglesa, principalmente nas circunstâncias específicas da área executiva. Para tanto, consideramos que não é suficiente ensinar apenas gramática e vocabulário. Assim, procuramos desenvolver todos os capítulos desta obra de modo a abordar diferentes gêneros textuais, recorrentes em diversas situações da área de negócios.

Visando à melhor compreensão por parte do aluno iniciante, alguns itens serão apresentados em português, mas, à medida que formos avançando nos capítulos, usaremos com mais frequência a língua inglesa.

Conceituação de inglês instrumental (*English for Specific Purposes* – ESP)

No Brasil, o projeto de inglês instrumental surgiu na Pontifícia Universidade Católica de São Paulo (PUC-SP), em 1983, coordenado pela Professora Dra. Antonieta Celani[2], atendendo à demanda que as universidades brasileiras

---

[1] "A language which is used for communication between groups of people who speak different languages but which is not used between members of the same group" (Procter, 1995, p. 827).

[2] A referida professora era, então, coordenadora do Programa de Mestrado em Linguística Aplicada da PUC-SP.

apresentavam em ministrar cursos de inglês para áreas específicas. Vejamos as perguntas mais pontuais relacionadas a essa abordagem:

1. O que é inglês instrumental?

    No Brasil, há várias abordagens de ensino de língua inglesa, entre as quais a do inglês instrumental, que visa à compreensão e à interpretação de textos científicos e técnicos por meio de estratégias específicas de leitura.

2. Qual é o objeto de estudo da abordagem do inglês instrumental?

    Seu objeto de estudo é o texto científico ou técnico, cuja compreensão é possibilitada até mesmo ao aluno que tem pouca noção de inglês.

3. Como acontece o ensino de gramática na abordagem do inglês instrumental?

    O ensino da gramática restringe-se ao indispensável, sendo, frequentemente, associado ao texto. Enfatiza-se o estudo de cognatos, de afixos e das estruturas básicas da língua em pauta.

4. Quais são as habilidades abordadas no ensino de inglês instrumental?

    Embora o enfoque maior seja na leitura, na compreensão e na interpretação de textos, o desenvolvimento da escrita é tão necessário quanto o da oralidade e o da compreensão auditiva.

Primeiro passo para leitura e compreensão de textos

Considerando-se que são diversas as interferências que a leitura de um texto pode sofrer, há de se destacar, especialmente, que todos nós trazemos um conhecimento de mundo (oriundo de nossas experiências pessoais, exposições a diferentes meios de comunicação, estudos que já realizamos etc.) e que, muitas vezes, não estamos conscientes de que possuímos toda essa bagagem de informações. Por isso, quando entramos em contato com um texto em língua estrangeira, costumamos não levar esses aspectos em conta.

Sugerimos, então, que a leitura seja iniciada com uma investigação sobre o título do texto e as imagens que porventura possam estar presentes, relacionando-se tais detalhes ao conhecimento prévio que você tenha a respeito do assunto. Tal estratégia nos dá a impressão de que acontece um "encaixe" desse conhecimento prévio com o texto que está sendo lido, o que contribui para a compreensão deste.

Semelhança entre as línguas e ordem dos vocábulos nas sentenças

Outro ponto relevante a ser levado em conta é a semelhança entre as línguas quanto à grafia dos vocábulos, por exemplo. Apesar de o inglês ter origem anglo-saxônica, em virtude da influência causada pela invasão romana ao Reino Unido da Grã Bretanha, nessa língua está presente também um grande número de vocábulos originados do latim, que, consequentemente, mantêm certa semelhança com o português.

A seguinte oração é um exemplo disso: *Miss Smith, the secretary of the sales manager received a fax changing the date of the visit*. Em português, seria: *Srta. Smith, a secretária do gerente de vendas recebeu um fax mudando a data da visita*.

Na oração citada, a dificuldade que poderia existir em relação à compreensão do verbo *change* seria superada com o auxílio de nosso conhecimento prévio de mundo, ou seja, poderíamos lembrar que tal verbo está presente nas casas de câmbio e nos bancos, significando "troca".

Outro ponto importante diz respeito à ordem dos vocábulos na organização da sentença. Em ambas as línguas, os vocábulos obedecem a uma ordem normal constituída por:

> Sujeito + Verbo + Complemento

Observemos, mais uma vez, a sentença:
» The secretary of the sales manager received a fax changing the date of the visit.
>> **Sujeito**: Miss Smith, the secretary of the sales manager.
>> **Verbo**: received.
>> **Complemento**: a fax changing the date of the visit.

Como podemos observar, a língua inglesa não é tão difícil quanto parece. Há, porém, alguns obstáculos que podem impedir a compreensão e que, consequentemente, devem ser levados em conta. Um deles relaciona-se a cognatos.

Conceituação de *cognato, skimming* e *scanning*

Para saber o que é um cognato, vamos analisar o que denominamos de *falso cognato*[3]. Falsos cognatos são palavras, geralmente de origem latina, que apresentam entre si certa semelhança ortográfica em duas línguas, mas que, com o passar dos anos, tiveram seus significados modificados. Vejamos um exemplo: *Actually, the library is opposite the bank*. Nessa frase, encontramos dois cognatos e dois falsos cognatos:

---

[3] Uma lista de falsos cognatos encontra-se nos apêndices ao final do livro.

» **Cognatos**: *opposite*, que significa "oposto", ou "do lado oposto", semelhantemente ao português; e *bank*, que significa "banco".
» **Falsos cognatos**: *actually*, que parece significar "atualmente", mas significa "realmente"; e *library*, que parece significar "livraria", mas quer dizer "biblioteca".

Ler um texto em língua estrangeira, assim como desenvolver qualquer outra habilidade, exige prática. Ser um bom leitor significa ler eficiente e rapidamente, alcançando a máxima compreensão, com o objetivo de captar, a princípio, as ideias gerais do autor e de, posteriormente, entender as informações mais específicas ou detalhadas. Esses processos, respectivamente, são chamados de *skimming* e *scanning*.

Mais especificamente, chamamos de *skimming* a primeira (e rápida) leitura, realizada para identificar o tema e a ideia geral do texto. Já *scanning* se relaciona à habilidade de encontrar informações mais detalhadas e/ou específicas, em uma leitura que não é, necessariamente, linear.

Exercise

1. Observe as sentenças a seguir e assinale **V** para *verdadeiro*, **F** para *falso* e **NS** para *não sei*:

   a) ( ) Ser um bom leitor significa ler cada letra de uma palavra e palavra por palavra de todas as sentenças de um texto.
   b) ( ) É necessário que saibamos o significado de cada palavra em uma sentença para compreendê-la completamente.
   c) ( ) Devemos sempre consultar o dicionário para descobrir o significado das palavras desconhecidas.
   d) ( ) A compreensão de qualquer texto só é possível quando entendemos todas as palavras nele contidas.
   e) ( ) Diferentes tipos de texto, como, receitas e jornais, são lidos da mesma maneira.
   f) ( ) Não é necessário o uso de nosso conhecimento intrínseco de mundo quando lemos um texto.

Como lemos?

Antes de ler o primeiro texto, vamos examinar o processo de leitura (*the reading process*). Reflita sobre as respostas que você marcou no *Exercise 1*. Note que nenhuma delas pode ser considerada verdadeira. Ter esse entendimento significa estar no caminho certo para se tornar um bom leitor de língua estrangeira. Todas as afirmativas apresentadas apontam para o modo como **não** se deve proceder diante de um texto.

Na realidade, um bom leitor compreende os processos envolvidos na leitura e os controla conscientemente. Essa habilidade, denominada *metacognição*, significa "saber sobre o saber". Quando conseguimos unir a metacognição à leitura, tornamo-nos bons leitores, ou seja, entendemos a ideia geral e assimilamos os detalhes por meio de um modelo cognitivo mais abrangente.

Com essas informações em mente, passemos, então, ao nosso primeiro texto.

Five strategies for good readers

1) Predict – Make guesses.
Good readers make predictions which may be confirmed or not. If they are proved invalid, you make new predictions. This constant process helps you to learn.

2) Picture – Form images.
For good readers, the words and the ideas on the page produce mental images. It helps you understand what you read.

3) Relate – Draw comparisons.
Comparing your experience to the new information in the text helps you understand the new material.

4) Monitor – Check comprehension.
Monitor your comprehension and try to resolve difficulties when they occur; do not continue reading when you are confused.

5) Correct – Find gaps in understanding.
If you have questions, stop and solve the problem. Find solutions, not confusion; if necessary, go back to a previous page for clarification.

Exercises

2. Qual é a ideia geral do texto?
   a) A importância de sempre formarmos imagens mentais ao lermos um texto.
   b) A importância da comparação para a compreensão de um texto.
   c) Estratégias que são úteis para uma boa leitura.
   d) Monitorar constantemente a compreensão de um texto é a melhor estratégia.

> Por meio do método de *skimming*, é possível encontrar a ideia geral do texto, apenas com a leitura do título "Five strategies for good readers". Logo, pode-se concluir que o texto refere-se a estratégias que podem ser utilizadas para realizar uma boa leitura.

3. Relacione os cognatos a seguir com os respectivos significados:
   a) strategies   ( ) clarificação
   b) process   ( ) comparação
   c) images   ( ) compreensão
   d) difficulties ( ) dificuldades

e) experience ( ) experiência
f) comparison ( ) imagens
g) clarification ( ) informação
h) solution ( ) processo
i) comprehension ( ) solução
j) information ( ) estratégias

4. O texto a seguir trata sobre a carreira de um administrador de empresas. Nele há vários vocábulos destacados. Leia o texto e responda à pergunta que o segue:

Business Administration professionals **have** a well-rounded education, so they **work** and **function** well in many different areas of a company or organization. The majority of those that **enter** into business administration **begin** as a department manager. This professional usually **plans**, **organizes**, and **controls** the overall duties of their assigned department. A typical organization generally has specific departments for sales, manufacturing, accounting, and finance. Each department **works** in cooperation with the next and communication **is** very important for the success of each department.

No texto, os vocábulos destacados são:

a) substantivos.
b) adjetivos.
c) verbos.
d) preposições.

> A resposta certa é a opção "c", verbos, pois estamos nos referindo a verdades universais e ações rotineiras de um profissional da área de administração de empresas. Ao falarmos de verdades e de rotina, geralmente usamos o *Simple Present*.

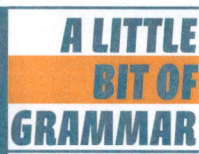

Verbos

São palavras que indicam uma **ação**, **condição** ou **experiência**. Podemos dividi-los em: verbos auxiliares (*auxiliary verbs*) e verbos principais (*main verbs*).

Auxiliary verbs

Be, *do* e *have* são verbos auxiliares que fornecem informações sobre o tempo em que o verbo principal se encontra. O verbo *be* é usado como auxiliar nos tempos contínuos (*Present, Past* e *Future Continuous*), e o verbo *have* é usado como auxiliar nos tempos perfeitos (*Present, Past* e *Future Perfect*).

O verbo auxiliar *do* é utilizado para:

» Fazer perguntas no presente – *To ask questions in the present*:
  › **Do** you like English? (Present)
  › **Does** your teacher speak French? (Present)

» Em sentenças negativas no presente – *For negative sentences in the present*:
   › It **doesn't** matter. (does + not = Present)
   › I **don't** play the piano. (do + not = Present)

Vejamos os três verbos auxiliares conjugados:

Chart 1.1 – The auxiliary verb ***be*** (ser, estar)

	Singular		Plural	
Affirmative	I	am	We	are
	He/She/It	is	You	are
	You	are	They	are

	Singular		Plural	
Interrogative	Am	I?	Are	we?
	Is	he/she/it?	Are	you?
	Are	you?	Are	they?

	Singular			Plural		
Negative	I	am not		We	are not	(aren't)
	He/She/It	is not	(isn't)	You	are not	(aren't)
	You	are not	(aren't)	They	are not	(aren't)

Chart 1.2 – The auxiliary verb ***have***[4] (ter)

	Singular		Plural	
Affirmative	I	have	We	have
	He/She/It	has	You	have
	You	have	They	have

	Singular		Plural	
Interrogative	Have	I?	Have	we?
	Has	he/she/it?	Have	you?
	Have	you?	Have	they?

	Singular			Plural		
Negative	I	have not	(haven't)	We	have not	(haven't)
	He/She/It	is not	(isn't)	You	have not	(haven't)
	You	are not	(aren't)	They	have not	(haven't)

---

[4] O verbo *have* também pode ser principal e, como tal, segue as regras de um verbo normal nas formas *interrogative* e *negative*. Ou seja, quando o *have* funciona como principal, utiliza-se o *do* como auxiliar, da mesma forma como se faz com os outros verbos.

Chart 1.3 – The auxiliary verb ***do***

Affirmative	Singular		Plural	
	I	do	We	do
	He/She/It	does	You	do
	You	do	They	do

Interrogative	Singular		Plural	
	Do	I?	Do	we?
	Does	he/she/it?	Do	you?
	Do	you?	Do	they?

Negative	Singular			Plural		
	I	do not	(don't)	We	do not	(don't)
	He/She/It	does not	(doesn't)	You	do not	(don't)
	You	do not	(don't)	They	do not	(don't)

Main verbs

Os outros verbos (ou seja, os verbos que não são auxiliares e, sim, principais) precisam do verbo auxiliar (*auxiliary verb*) em frases interrogativas e negativas. Vejamos alguns exemplos:

Chart 1.4 – Main verbs in the ***Simple Present***.

Affirmative

I / You / We / They	understand English.	He / She / It	understands English.

Interrogative

Do	I / You / We / They	understand English?	Does	He / She / It	understand English?

Negative

I / You / We / They	do not (don't) understand English.	He / She / It	does not (doesn't) understand English.

Lembre-se

» No presente (*Simple Present*), na terceira pessoa do singular (*he, she, it*), adiciona-se **s** ao final da maioria dos verbos (*like**s**, play**s**, work**s**, see**s**, look**s***).
» Para verbos com terminações em *o, sh, ch, s, z*, adiciona-se **es** (*do**es**, wash**es**, watch**es**, dress**es**, buzz**es***).
» Para verbos que terminam em *y* precedido de consoante, retira-se o *y* e adiciona-se ***ies*** (*cry/cr**ies**, fly/fl**ies***).

Advérbios

É comum usar o presente simples (*Simple Present*) com advérbios de frequência, uma vez que essa classe gramatical está relacionada a ações habituais, rotineiras. Por exemplo:

» I **usually** meet all the sales staff. (Eu **normalmente** encontro todos os vendedores)

Os advérbios mais usuais são: *never, rarely = seldom = hardly ever, sometimes, often = frequently, usually* e *always*.

Exercise

5. Relacione as duas colunas de acordo com o significado dos advérbios (*match the columns*):

a) generally   (   ) ocasionalmente
b) ever   (   ) raramente
c) occasionally (   ) quinzenalmente
d) once   (   ) quase nunca, raramente
e) seldom   (   ) repetidamente
f) regularly   (   ) geralmente
g) repeatedly   (   ) alguma vez
h) hardly ever   (   ) todo dia
i) twice   (   ) regularmente
j) every day   (   ) duas vezes
k) fortnightly   (   ) uma vez
l) once in a while (   ) de vez em quando

Um ponto interessante a ser observado é que, assim como a maioria dos advérbios em português termina em *-mente*, a maioria dos advérbios em inglês termina em *-ly*.

A posição dos advérbios nas sentenças

Observe os seguintes exemplos:
» The boss is **always** on time.
» The boss **never** arrives late.

De acordo com esses exemplos, podemos notar que:
» advérbios de frequência são posicionados **depois** do verbo *to be*;
» esses mesmos advérbios são posicionados **antes** de outros verbos.

> Chamamos a atenção para o fato de que adotaremos, em todos os capítulos, um procedimento metodológico denominado *Presentation, Practice, Production* (PPP). Em outras palavras, apresentaremos o conteúdo a ser desenvolvido na unidade (*Presentation*); a seguir, trabalharemos com a fixação da aprendizagem por meio de exercícios práticos repetitivos (*Practice*); e, por último, com base nesses dois passos anteriores, daremos a você a oportunidade de produzir o conteúdo aprendido por meio de textos e exercícios mais comunicativos (*Production*).

Exercises

6. Give a negative and then a positive answer. Follow the pattern:

   Are you a teacher? (university student)
   No, I am not. I am a university student.

   a) Is this a book? (notebook)

   b) Are you American? (Brazilian)

   c) Are you and Mary students? (secretaries)

   d) Is John a teacher? (manager)

   e) Is this a new computer? (an old)

   f) Are Mary and Jane sisters? (co-workers)

   g) Are Paul and John the new directors ? (new managers)

   h) Is Peter the assistant? (office boy)

7. **Read the following text:**

   a) Complete the passage with verbs in the Simple Present, affirmative or negative, according to the information in parentheses:

   Mary _____ (**be**) a bank manager. Every morning she _____ (**get**) up at 6 a.m., _____ (**take**) a shower, _____ (**get**) dressed, _____ (**have**) breakfast and _____ (**go**) to work at 7:15 a.m. She usually _____ (**arrive**) at the office at about 7:50 a.m. because she _____ (**start**) working at 8:00 o'clock. Twice a week, she _____ (**have**) lunch with her friends at an Italian restaurant near the bank. She _____ (**have** – neg.) lunch at home as she _____ (**live**) a bit far from her job. Sometimes she _____ (**work** – neg.) in the bank in the afternoon because she _____ (**have**) meetings with the clients outside the company. Due to the rush hour, she _____ (**go** – neg.) back home by bus, she often _____ (**return**) home in the evening by subway.

   b) Copy the completed text above using the first person (singular) and make all the necessary changes. Remember to use *I* and *my* instead of *she* and *her* (*eu* e *meu/minha* no lugar de *ela/dela*):

   _____
   _____
   _____
   _____
   _____
   _____
   _____
   _____
   _____
   _____

8. You are interested in your friend's routine and decide to ask him/her if, for example, he/she usually goes to the bank (Você está interessado(a) na rotina de seu(sua) amigo(a) e decide perguntar-lhe se, por exemplo, ele/ela normalmente vai ao banco):

   Do you usually go to the bank?
     (Você normalmente vai ao banco?)

   Now continue the same way:

   a) He/she uses the computer every day.
   _____

b) He/she usually sends e-mails.
_____

c) He/she often has appointments.
_____

d) He/she sometimes interviews new employees.
_____

e) He/she always writes reports.
_____

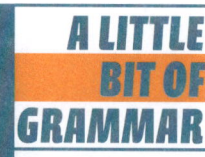

Short answers

Em um diálogo, é muito comum que o receptor responda às perguntas do emissor por meio do uso de respostas curtas. Certamente é possível utilizar respostas maiores e mais bem elaboradas, mas, primeiramente, veremos como usar respostas curtas.

Quando a pergunta se inicia pelo auxiliar *do/does*, usamos as seguintes respostas:

Yes, I do.	Yes, you do.	Yes, he/ she/ it does.
No, I don't.	No, you don't.	No, he/ she/ it doesn't
Yes, we do.	Yes, they do.	
No, we don't.	No, they don't.	

Exercise

9. Answer the questions from *Exercise 8* using short answers, according to your routine. Follow the example:

Do you usually go to the bank?
    Yes, I do./No, I don't.

a) _____

b) _____

c) _____

d) _____

e) _____

Greetings (cumprimentos)

Os cumprimentos são bastante comuns na língua inglesa, mas as maneiras como as pessoas se cumprimentam variam, dependendo do que chamamos (linguisticamente) de *registro*, ou seja, dependendo da formalidade ou informalidade de cada ocasião. Como o mundo dos negócios exige um registro mais formal, vamos iniciar por esse tipo de cumprimento.

Formal greetings

É educado saudar e responder à saudação de acordo com as seguintes orientações:
- **Good morning** – de manhã.
- **Good afternoon** – de tarde, até aproximadamente às 18h.
- **Good evening** – de noite, ao encontrar alguém.
- **Good night** – de noite, ao se despedir ou ao se deitar.

Informal greetings

Há várias maneiras de saudar alguém, dependendo da familiaridade entre as pessoas. Em uma situação informal, a qualquer hora do dia, os americanos preferem usar *Hi* para saudar e, também, para responder à saudação. Já os britânicos, de modo geral, preferem *Hi there* ou *Hello* para ambas as situações, saudar e responder.

Outras maneiras também podem ser usadas, tais como:
- **How are you doing?**
- **What's up?**
- **How are you?**

Vale ressaltar que não é sempre necessário responder a essas três últimas saudações. Se forem respondidas, no entanto, as opções seguintes são as mais frequentemente utilizadas:
- **Fine!**
- **Great!**
- **Not too bad!**

Introductions

Existem várias maneiras de nos apresentarmos e/ou sermos apresentados, dependendo do grau de formalidade entre as pessoas em questão. Em uma situação formal, as duas pessoas costumam dizer: ***How do you do?***

Apesar de a oração parecer estranha, trata-se de uma curiosidade da língua inglesa, como no diálogo a seguir:

> **Mrs. Smith**: Mr. Green, I would like to introduce you to the new manager, Mr. Brown.
> **Mr. Green** responds: How do you do?
> **Mr. Brown** replies: How do you do?

Em uma situação não tão formal, o diálogo poderia ser da seguinte maneira:

> **Mrs. Smith**: Mr. Green, I would like to introduce you to the new manager, Mr. Brown.

Mr. Green responds: It's a pleasure to meet you, Mr. Brown.
Mr. Brown replies: It's a pleasure to meet you too.

Uma terceira opção também seria possível:

Mrs Smith: Mr. Green, I would like to introduce you to the new manager, Mr. Brown.
Mr. Green responds: Pleased to meet, Mr. Brown.
Mr. Brown replies: Pleased to meet you too.

Por outro lado, quando se trata de uma situação bastante informal, como entre dois secretários, são comuns as seguintes opções:

Maria: Hello, I'm Maria.
ou
Hello, my name's Maria.

Peter: Hi, I'm Peter.
ou
Hello, Maria, I'm Peter
ou
Nice to meet you, I'm Peter.

EXPLORING vocabulary

Um fator importante para o domínio de um idioma estrangeiro é a aquisição de vocabulário geral e, sobretudo, específico para a sua área de interesse – no nosso caso, *the business field*. Há várias maneiras de se adquirir vocabulário, e uma delas é por meio de associações recorrentes de palavras, ou seja, colocações (*collocations*).

Essas associações fundamentam-se na frequência em que certas palavras são usadas em união com outras. Por exemplo, quando viajamos de avião, devemos apertar o cinto de segurança. O verbo *apertar* em inglês pode ser *to tighten* ou *to fasten*. No entanto, tomando como base a frequência de uso da expressão, podemos afirmar que a colocação adequada seria *Fasten your seatbelts*. Lembramos que a expressão *Tighten your seatbelts* poderia ser compreendida, mas não seria usada pelos falantes nativos da língua.

> Em razão da importância do conhecimento não apenas de palavras isoladas, mas também de colocações, incluiremos, ao final de cada capítulo, alguns exercícios voltados para a aquisição de vocabulário.

Exercise Approaching Collocations

10. Match the words on the right with the ones on the left to build collocations (No word should be left out):

a) pleasure   ( ) the computer
b) use   ( ) to meet you
c) send   ( ) an appointment
d) interview   ( ) an e-mail
e) have   ( ) candidates
f) rush   ( ) morning
g) every   ( ) staff
h) sales   ( ) hour
i) how   ( ) bye
j) good   ( ) do you do?

Síntese do capítulo

No presente capítulo, abordamos a relevância do conhecimento da língua inglesa no ambiente profissional. Examinamos os primeiros passos indispensáveis para a leitura e a compreensão de textos, enfatizando a importância da utilização de técnicas de leitura, tais como a observação da semelhança entre as línguas em pauta, a ordem dos vocábulos nas sentenças, os conhecimentos pessoais de mundo, o reconhecimento de cognatos e de falsos cognatos e o uso de *skimming* e *scanning*. No que concerne à gramática, investigamos os verbos no presente e os advérbios de frequência. Em seguida, observando o ciclo PPP, apresentamos vários tipos diferentes de exercícios para fixação, bem como curiosidades a respeito da língua e dos costumes dos países de língua inglesa.

Organizar e administrar o tempo

Saber administrar o tempo é importante em qualquer profissão, mas é algo essencial para quem trabalha em um ambiente empresarial. Isso porque, nos dias de hoje, há um acúmulo de atribuições que transformam a rotina de trabalho em um caos total, caso não saibamos nos organizar.

Na visão do pesquisador Alberto Alvarães[1] (2012), administração de tempo não é uma técnica, mas um comportamento, uma atitude que deve ser tomada diante de uma determinada tarefa. Certamente, o uso adequado de uma agenda que sirva de apoio é de grande valia, pois essa ferramenta contribui para o gerenciamento do nosso tempo, evitando os percalços da desorganização. A rima a seguir ilustra o que acontece quando há falta de planejamento organizacional:

> When you know how to manage your time, you gain control,
>
> Rather than busily working here, there and everywhere
>
> And not getting much done anywhere.
>
> (Mind Tools, 2009)

Agenda

Em inglês, podemos usar os termos *diary* e *organiser* para nos referirmos à agenda, objeto que é imprescindível para o bom andamento de nossas atividades diárias. Lembramos que o tempo verbal normalmente aplicado nas anotações feitas em agendas é o *imperativo*, como podemos observar no exemplo a seguir, da agenda de Mary Smith, advogada na empresa C&H Enterprises:

---

[1] O referido pesquisador é um renomado professor, mestre e consultor em gestão de pessoas. Aborda o tema "cultura, clima e comportamento organizacional", entre outros, no *site* <https://sites.google.com/site/profalbertoalvaraes>.

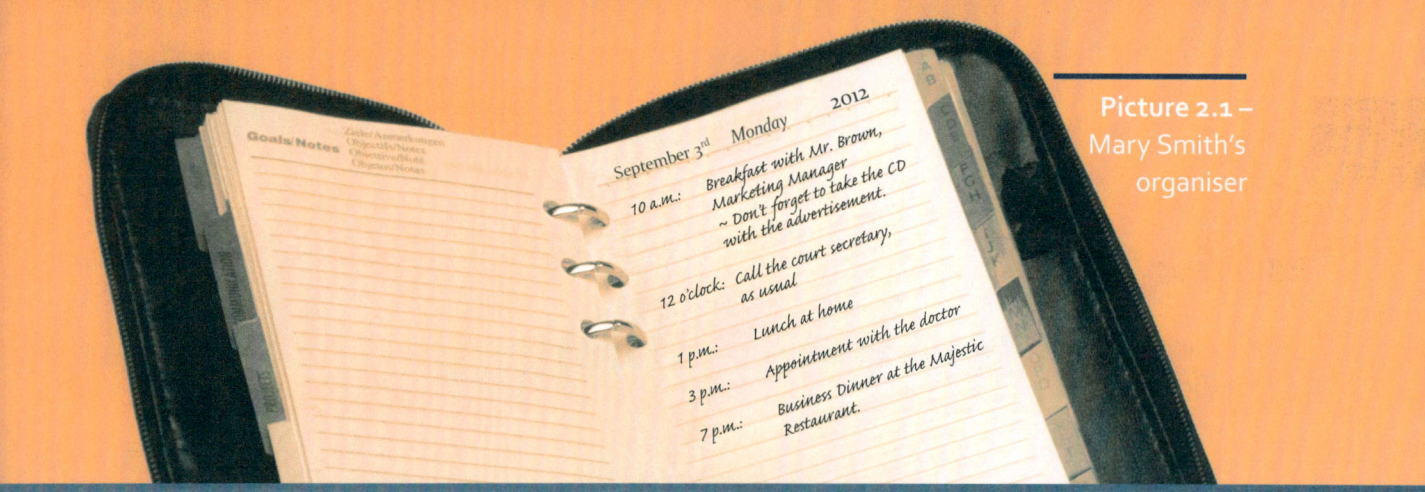

Picture 2.1 – Mary Smith's organiser

Ao fazermos anotações e pedidos e ao darmos ordens, geralmente usamos o imperativo (afirmativo ou negativo). No imperativo afirmativo, simplesmente usamos o infinitivo do verbo sem a partícula *to*, como na frase *Call the court secretary, as ususal*. No negativo, inserimos o auxiliar *don't* antes do verbo em questão, como em *Don't forget to take the CD with the advertisement!*

Na sequência, vamos conhecer os pronomes interrogativos para que você possa, posteriormente, responder a algumas perguntas sobre a agenda apresentada.

A LITTLE BIT OF GRAMMAR

WH questions

- » **What** (O que)
  - › What do you do?
  - › I am a university student.

- » **Where** (Onde/A-onde)
  - › Where do you study?
  - › I study at Uninter.

- » **When** (Quando)
  - › When do you read your personal e-mails?
  - › I read them when I have free time.

- » **Who** (Quem)
  - › Who is your manager?
  - › Mr. Smith is my manager.

- » **Why** (Por que)
  - › Why are you a clerk?
  - › I am a clerk because I think it is a good job.

- » **Whose** (De quem)
  - › Whose office is that?
  - › It is the manager's office.

- » **Which** (Qual)
  - › Which schedule do you prefer: morning or afternoon?
  - › I prefer the morning.

» **How** (Como)
  › How do you come to work?
  › I usually come to work by car.

Exercise

1. Look at Mary Smith's organiser (Picture 2.1) and answer the following questions:
   a) Is Mary free this morning?

   b) Who does she have breakfast with?

   c) What does she need to take to the meeting with the marketing manager?

   d) At what time does she usually call the court secretary?

   e) Is she free in the afternoon?

   f) Who does she have an appointment with in the afternoon?

   g) What about evenings? Is she free in the evening?

   h) What is her appointment for the evening?

Como o gênero textual trabalhado neste capítulo é a agenda, acreditamos ser necessário recordar o vocabulário mais recorrente nesse tipo de texto: os dias da semana, os meses do ano, os números e as horas.

» **The days of the week**
  › On **Sundays** we go to church.
  › The secretary often buys office supplies on **Mondays**.
  › My assistant usually books my business trips on **Tuesdays**.
  › **Wednesday** is the meeting day.
  › I generally send reports to the manager on **Thursdays**.
  › On **Fridays** everybody wears casual clothes.
  › We sometimes do shift work on **Saturdays**.

Chamamos a atenção para o fato de que, em inglês, os dias da semana e os meses do ano devem ser escritos iniciados com letra maiúscula.

» **The seasons and the months of the year**

Summer
› In **December** we have a Christmas party at the company.
› Many employees take vacation in **January**.
› We have a lot of free time in **February** because of Carnival.

Autumn/Fall
› The weather in **March** is usually rainy and windy.
› The leaves fall from the trees in **April**.
› We celebrate Labor Day on the first of **May**.

Winter
› We always have *Festa Junina* at the company in **June**.
› Some employees prefer to take vacation in **July** because their children are off school.
› **August** is a very busy month at the company.

Spring
› In **September** we have two important events: Independence Day and Secretary's day.
› In **October** we often have a Halloween party at the company.
› We start the preparations for the New Year's Eve in **November**.

Prepositions

Destacamos que as preposições relativas aos dias da semana são diferentes daquelas usadas nos meses do ano, bem como as usadas para indicar as estações. Isto é, para os dias da semana, a preposição correta é *on*; já para os meses do ano e para as estações, devemos usar a preposição *in*, conforme pode ser observado nos exemplos citados.

Exercise

2. Answer the questions:

   a) What is your favorite day?
   _____

   b) When do we have winter vacation in the USA?
   _____

   c) What is considered a business week?
   _____

   d) Do you have shift work in your company?
   _____

   e) In which month do you celebrate your birthday?
   _____

Numbers

Agora, vamos trabalhar com os números cardinais e ordinais.

Chart 2.1 – Numbers from 1 to 31

Cardinal numbers	Ordinal numbers
1 – one	1st – first
2 – two	2nd – second
3 – three	3rd – third
4 – four	4th – fourth
5 – five	5th – fifth
6 – six	6th – sixth
7 – seven	7th – seventh
8 – eight	8th – eighth
9 – nine	9th – ninth
10 – ten	10th – tenth
11 – eleven	11th – eleventh
12 – twelve	12th – twelfth
13 – thirteen	13th – thirteenth
14 – fourteen	14th – fourteenth
15 – fifteen	15th – fifteenth
16 – sixteen	16th – sixteenth
17 – seventeen	17th – seventeenth
18 – eighteen	18th – eighteenth
19 – nineteen	19th – nineteenth
20 – twenty	20th – twentieth
21 – twenty-one	21st – twenty-first
22 – twenty-two	22nd – twenty-second

(continua)

Chart 2.1 – (conclusão)

Cardinal numbers	Ordinal numbers
23 – twenty-three	23rd – twenty-third
24 – twenty-four	24th – twenty-fourth
25 – twenty-five	25th – twenty-fifth
26 – twenty-six	26th – twenty-sixth
27 – twenty-seven	27th – twenty-seventh
28 – twenty-eight	28th – twenty-eighth
29 – twenty-nine	29th – twenty-ninth
30 – thirty	30th – thirtieth
31 – thirty-one	31st – thirty-first

Como você pode observar, os números ordinais *first*, *second* e *third* têm terminações diferentes, sendo, respectivamente, *st*, *nd* e *rd*, que são as letras acrescentadas a esses três numerais para indicar sua forma abreviada. De *fourth* a *twentieth*, a terminação é *th* – logo, acrescenta-se a esses numerais o *th*, para abreviá-los. Depois de *twenty-first*, diferentemente da língua portuguesa, modifica-se apenas o último algarismo da direita. Por exemplo: Hoje é Natal, dia 25 de dezembro – *Today is Christmas, the twenty-fifth (25th of December)*.

Datas

Lembramos que, em inglês, os ordinais são usados em várias situações, como nos casos em que queremos expressar datas e quando nos referimos aos andares de um edifício:
 » Christmas is on December 25th (December twenty-fifth).
 » Christmas is on 25th December (the twenty-fifth of December).
 » My office is on the 10th (tenth) floor.

Outro ponto importante é a leitura dos anos. Lemos até o ano 1999 dividindo os números em dois. Por exemplo, o ano 1999 é lido como *nineteen ninety-nine*. Já o ano 2000, lemos *two thousand*, e assim por diante. Vejamos um exemplo:
 » Brasil became independent from Portugal on **7th September, 1822**.
    › **The seventh of September, eighteen twenty-two.**
    ou
    › **September seventh, eighteen twenty-two.**

What time is it? What's the time?

It's nine o'clock.

It's nine 0 five (lê-se como a letra o); it's five past nine.

It's nine ten; it's ten past nine.

It's nine fifteen; it's fifteen past nine; it's a quarter after nine.

It's nine twenty; it's twenty past nine.

It's nine twenty five; it's twenty five past nine.

It's nine thirty; it's half past nine.

It's nine thirty five; it's twenty five to ten.

It's nine forty; it's twenty to ten.

It's nine forty five; it's fifteen to ten; it's a quarter to ten.

It's nine fifty; it's ten to ten.

It's nine fifty five; it's five to ten.

It's ten o'clock.

A LITTLE BIT OF GRAMMAR

Present Continuous/Present Progressive

Quando queremos expressar uma ação que está acontecendo no momento atual, usamos o *Present Continuous*, também denominado *Present Progressive*. Esse tempo verbal é formado da seguinte maneira:

> Sujeito + verbo *to be* + verbo principal no infinitivo + *ing*

Observe os exemplos a seguir:

» **Listen! The telephone is ringing.**
   › Sujeito: the telephone
   › Verbo auxiliar *to be*: is
   › Verbo principal no infinitivo + *ing*: *ringing*

» **Office hours start at 9 a.m. It's nine o'clock now. They are starting their work.**
   › Sujeito: They
   › Verbo auxiliar *to be*: are
   › Verbo principal no infinitivo + *ing*: *starting*

O *Present Continuous* também pode ser usado para indicar uma ação em um futuro próximo, previamente planejado, como na frase a seguir:

» **They aren't connecting it until this afternoon.**

Exercises

3. No diálogo a seguir, duas técnicas de suporte à internet conversam ao telefone. Identifique e sublinhe o *Present Continuous* que elas utilizam durante a conversa:

Miss Smith: Good morning. It's Miss Smith speaking.
Miss Brown: Good morning, this is Miss Brown. How are you doing?
Miss Smith: Fine, thanks. And you?
Miss Brown: Not bad, thanks.
Miss Smith: Miss Brown, is the Internet working ok on your floor?
Miss Brown: No, it is not working today. We are having problems with the connection. Why?
Miss Smith: Well, the director needs the Internet to take part in a video conference and he can't wait for a long time to have it connected. I thought the problem could be only on my floor.
Miss Brown: Sorry, but this problem is everywhere in the country today.
Miss Smith: All right. Do you have any idea of when the connection will be ok again?

Miss Brown: They aren't connecting it until this afternoon, unfortunately.
Miss Smith: All right. Thank you very much for your help. Bye.
Miss Brown: Welcome and good-bye.

4. Note que as duas técnicas acima usam o *Present Continuous* para fazer perguntas. Agora, complete a regra referente à forma interrogativa desse tempo verbal:

   _____ + sujeito + verbo + _____?

5. Observe também que Miss Brown usa o *Present Continuous* na forma negativa. Complete a regra referente a essa forma:

   Sujeito + _____ not + verbo + _____.

A LITTLE BIT OF READING

How to choose your profession

In the past it was quite easy to choose a profession. Today it is more difficult because of three main reasons:
- » There are more professions available.
- » Career definitions are in constant change.
- » People today have more expectations about their professions.

Men and women entering the work force now expect to change their careers three or more times during their lives, so here are some steps to help you to choose your career in a more conscious manner.

To have better chances of getting a good job, what you have to do is:

Consider what you like.

Think about what you really enjoy doing. This will help you understand your values, which is important when choosing a career.

Identify your abilities.

Abilities are skills and talents. A skill is something you learn and a talent is something you are born with.

Identify your preferences.

We all have preferences which influence the way we function with others. It is relevant to identify these preferences because it will help you to choose your profession.

Experiment.

If you don't have any experience, talk to people and try to learn from them.

Money is important, but it is not everything in life.

If possible, try to choose a career in which you may grow. This may not be the one which pays you the best initial salary.

Become 110% committed.

To grow, you have to be involved 110% in what you are doing or do something else.

Adapt your lifestyle to your salary, not your expectations.

Do not spend all your salary. Structure your lifestyle so you can always keep part of your payment. To accumulate money, it is important to start saving early and to invest regularly.

Study, have objectives and face challenges.

Always dedicate some time to study and have that great objective to achieve. If necessary, change or adapt to new conditions. Finally, face challenges!

Exercises

6. The main idea of the passage is:
   a) How to change your job effectively.
   b) How to choose a suitable career.
   c) How to resign from your job.
   d) For career improvement, give priority to experience.

7. According to the text, identify the sentences as true (T) or false (F):
   ( ) Values, skills, talents, preferences and goal setting
       are essential in today's business's world.
   ( ) Commitment is one of the most important features
       to consider when choosing a career.
   ( ) Prioritize your salary, but spend your money to live well.
   ( ) Avoid having a narrow-minded vision
       when entering the workforce.
   a) F, F, F, T.
   b) F, F, T, T.
   c) T, T, F, T.
   d) T, T, T, T.

8. According to the text, which is a good way to get experience?
   a) Always set a goal.
   b) Never stop studying.
   c) Talk to a lot of people and try to get knowledge from them.
   d) Choose the profession that offers you the best salary.

A LITTLE BIT OF GRAMMAR

Pronomes demonstrativos

Há quatro pronomes demonstrativos na língua inglesa. Para usá-los de um modo mais efetivo, devemos considerar sempre a distância entre o falante e o objeto demonstrado.

Chart 2.2 – Demonstrative pronouns

	Singular	Plural
Near you (perto de você)	This	These
Far from you (longe de você)	That	Those

Exercise

9. Read the passage about "choosing a career" again, find examples of demonstrative pronouns and copy the sentences in the lines provided:

    a) _____

    b) _____

    c) _____

Simple Present × Present Continuous (Progressive)

Antes de prosseguirmos, vamos rever os tempos verbais aprendidos até o momento e comparar seus usos:

Chart 2.3 – Simple Present and Present Continuous (Progressive)

	Affirmative	Interrogative	Negative
Simple Present	You study.	Do you study?	I don't study.
	She studies.	Does she study?	She doesn't study.
Present Continuous (Progressive)	You are studying.	Are you studying?	You aren't studying.
	She is studying.	Is she studying?	She isn't studying.

Assim como na língua portuguesa, na inglesa há dois tipos de presente. Usamos o *Simple Present* para descrever ações habituais e rotineiras e para expressar verdades universais e o *Present Continuous* para descrever ações que estão acontecendo no momento da fala e ações já planejadas no futuro.

Exercises

10. Escreva *right* quando as sentenças estiverem corretas e *wrong* se achar que há algum erro. A seguir, reescreva as que estiverem marcadas com *wrong*, corrigindo-as:

    a) Look! The sun shines.
    _____

    b) I am getting tired. Let's go home.
    _____

c) Mr. Smith's secretary is writing e-mails every morning.
_____

d) Miss Brown is coming for the appointment tomorrow at 9.
_____

e) — Where do you go?
— I am going shopping for supplies.
_____
_____

11. **Complete the sentences using the Simple Present or the Present Continuous:**

Example:

I always _____ golf on Saturday morning.

(x) play   ( ) plays   ( ) playing

a) Tom _____ the minutes of the meeting now.
( ) to type   ( ) is typing   ( ) types

b) Paul and Peter usually _____ lunch at work.
( ) have   ( ) haves   ( ) has

c) Diana often _____ to the dentist after work.
( ) go   ( ) goes   ( ) is going

d) Look! An airplane from the USA _____ at this moment.
( ) lands   ( ) is landing   ( ) are landing

e) We usually _____ good articles in this magazine.
( ) read   ( ) reads   ( ) are reading

f) The trains from Newcastle _____ late every day.
( ) arrives   ( ) is arriving   ( ) arrive

g) Be quiet! My boss _____ an important report.
( ) writes   ( ) write   ( ) is writing

h) They usually _____ at the club.
( ) swims   ( ) swim   ( ) are swimming

i) Tom always _____ all his salary before the end of the month.
( ) spends   ( ) spend   ( ) is spending

j) My brother _____ part of his salary every month.
( ) saves   ( ) is saving   ( ) save

12. Change the highlighted information to the information in parentheses, passing the sentences from the Simple Present to the Present Continuous:

   For example:
   She buys computer supplies **every week**. (now)
   She is buying computer supplies now.

   a) They go to the new branch **every year**. (now)

   b) He eats fish and chips **on Sundays**. (now)

   c) She orders chips **every meal**. (now)

   d) They live in England **every year**. (now)

   e) He writes **novels**. (dramas now)

   f) They drink **soft drinks** during the lunch. (water now)

   g) He assists **Anna at work**. (Paula now)

   h) She listens to the radio **at night**. (now)

   i) They play cards **every night**. (now)

13. Form sentences in the Simple Present or in the Present Continuous:

   a) The secretaries / to study / English / every day.

   b) The employees / to play / football / now.

   c) The secretary / to watch TV / now.

   d) We / to wash / hands / before meal / every day.

   e) The girls / to work / now.

   f) The teacher / to speak / English / now.

A LITTLE BIT OF READING

Seasons of the year

There are four seasons in the year and they are usually based on the weather. If you live in more northern or southern countries, then you probably have four seasons: **spring**, **summer**, **autumn** and **winter**. It is usually warm in the summer, and cold in the winter, but in some parts of the world the temperature doesn't change much. Near the equator, there is a rainy and a dry season. In some places there are also special seasons; for example, 'hurricane' season.

The USA are in the northern hemisphere of the planet. They have four very different seasons there: spring, summer, autumn and winter. Many countries in the northern hemisphere have four seasons, like Japan. In the United Kingdom, there are four seasons but the winter is not so cold, and the summer is not so hot.

In the southern hemisphere, many countries have four seasons too, but these countries have the seasons at different times. When it is summer in Japan, it is winter in Argentina. When it is winter in Japan, it is summer in Argentina.

Countries near the equator do not usually have different seasons. Temperatures are usually similar all year round, but many countries near the equator have wet and dry seasons. Singapore, for example, has two monsoon seasons when the country has more rain.

Of course light changes with the seasons too. On the equator, the length of days and nights doesn't change much, but as you move away from the equator the days and nights get longer in the summer and shorter in the winter. In the south of Norway, for example, there are 19 hours of daylight in the middle of summer, and only 5 hours in the middle of winter.

Exercise

14. After reading the text, please answer the following questions:

a) What are the seasons of the year?
___

b) Do all the countries in the world have the same seasons?
___

c) Do we have a monsoon season in Brazil?
___

d) What is your favorite season?
___

e) Are the summer months in Brazil the same as in the USA?
___

f) What are the winter months in Brazil?
_____

Curiosidades

Na língua inglesa, não existe o verbo *haver*. Para a forma afirmativa, usamos a expressão *there is* seguida de vocábulos no singular e a expressão *there are* seguida de vocábulos no plural. As formas interrogativa e negativa seguem as regras do verbo *to be*. Como você pode observar, no texto anterior, há exemplos de *there is* e de *there are*.

15. Localize os exemplos de *there is* e *there are* no texto anterior:

   a) _____
   b) _____
   c) _____
   d) _____

Curiosidades

O modo mais usual para identificarmos os períodos antes ou depois do meio-dia é com o uso das abreviações *a.m.* e *p.m.*, cujos significados são, respectivamente, *ante meridiem* (antes do meio-dia) e *post meridiem* (depois do meio-dia). Por exemplo:

   » Let's meet at 11 a.m. and go home at 5 p.m.

Entretanto, para indicar meio-dia, podemos usar as seguintes formas:

   » 12:00 – It's 12 o'clock p.m. / It's midday / It's noon.

Por outro lado, para a meia-noite, usamos apenas as duas formas a seguir:

   » 12:00 – It's 12 o'clock a.m. / It's midnight.

Exercise Approaching Collocations

16. Match the words on the right with the ones on the left to build collocations (no word should be left out):

   a) nice, rainy, cloudy, windy, sunny   ( ) range
   b) main   ( ) a career
   c) wide   ( ) reason
   d) work   ( ) weather
   e) set and reach   ( ) world
   f) business   ( ) vacation
   g) choose   ( ) into account
   h) take   ( ) force
   i) go on   ( ) an appointment, a meeting
   j) have   ( ) a goal

Síntese do capítulo

No presente capítulo, lidamos com a questão do tempo, abordando os aspectos lexicais pertinentes ao tema, bem como os seguintes tempos verbais: imperativo, presente simples e presente progressivo. Examinamos também os números cardinais, os ordinais e as várias maneiras possíveis de dizermos as horas. Usamos neste capítulo textos maiores, com o objetivo de possibilitar leituras e interpretações mais elaboradas e a aquisição de um vocabulário mais rico e de maior utilidade para o aumento gradual dos conhecimentos em língua inglesa.

Qualidade de vida no ambiente de trabalho 3

Visando ao desenvolvimento da leitura e à aquisição de maior vocabulário, vamos dar início a este novo capítulo com um exercício de compreensão de texto.

A LITTLE BIT OF READING

Quality of working life

According to the Financial Times Lexicon (QoWL, 2008), quality of working life expresses the feeling that an employee gets from his/her job and whether he/she feels happy or satisfied.

To check whether you have a high quality of working life, answer both questions from the following questionnaire:

1) How often do the following situations occur?

	Never	Seldom	Sometimes	Often	Always
a) I am sure about what is expected of me at work.					
b) I know how to get my job done.					
c) If work gets difficult, my colleagues help me.					
d) I have achievable deadlines.					
e) I am clear about what my duties and responsibilities are.					
f) If I am subject of bullying or personal harassment, I am sure I will have the suitable support from the company.					

(continua)

(conclusão)

2) To what extent do you agree with the following?

	Strongly disagree	Disagree	Neutral	Agree	Strongly agree
g) I receive the respect I deserve at work.					
h) I have opportunities to question managers about changes.					
i) My working time may be flexible to suit my personal life.					
j) I never feel under pressure at work.					
k) I have a clear set of goals and aims to motivate me to do my job well.					
l) I work in a safe environment.					

Source: Adapted from Qowl, 2008.

How to check your answers:

» If you have answered *always* to all the items in Question 1 and *strongly agree* to all the items in Question 2, congratulations!!!! You have an excellent quality of working life.
» If you have answered exactly the opposite, *never* and *strongly disagree*, you should try to find somewhere better to work.
» If you are somewhere in the middle, you should rethink your working life and see whether it is worthy working for this company.

Exercise

1. Which question mentions:
   a) Working time. ( )
   b) Set of goals. ( )
   c) Deadlines. ( )
   d) Bullying or harassment. ( )

Writing informal letters

Ao escrevermos cartas ou *e-mails* informais, devemos estar atentos ao registro adequado, isto é, devemos selecionar o vocabulário conveniente para uma situação que apresente certa informalidade. Em uma analogia, poderíamos dizer que, para ir ao cinema, não nos vestimos da maneira formal como fazemos quando vamos a um casamento, e vice-versa.

Vejamos a carta que Margareth escreveu a sua amiga Mary convidando-a para passar o Natal em sua nova residência e dando-lhe detalhes de sua melhor qualidade de vida.

183 Hill Lane,

London, UK.

20th July, 2007.

Dear Mary,

 Sorry, it's been so long since I last wrote, but I have been busy moving away and tidying the house. Well, how are things with you? Are you working too hard?
 Anyway, I'm writing because if you don't have any plans for **your** Christmas holidays this year, perhaps you would like to come and stay with us. The last time we met was two months ago, and both George and I would love to see you again. You know that we have a bigger house now, and there's plenty of room for one or two guests. In fact, we moved to the countryside ten days ago and we are really enjoying the village.
 George and I have a much better quality of life now because we have plenty of time to stretch **our** legs, breathe fresh air and relax taking the dog for a walk. Do you remember George had a terrible pain in the back? Well, **his** health is great now! **Mine** too because I stopped having that awful headache. Besides, my parents live near here, so we can go to **their** house for lunch on Sundays. **My** mother still has a problem in her feet, but she cooks very well.
 We also have a big garden now, though I think at Christmas time you'll be more interested in the central heating, which works very well, fortunately! Do come!
 We are all looking forward to seeing you.
 Much love from your friends,
 Margaret and George

Exercise

2. What is the main idea of the passage?
   a) To apologize for not writing before.
   b) To invite a friend to spend Christmas together.
   c) To invite the friend to see the new house.
   d) To invite the friend for lunch on Sunday.
   e) To tell the friend about the new house.

A LITTLE BIT OF GRAMMAR

The Simple Past

Observe que, na carta anterior, Margareth escreve sobre algumas situações que aconteceram, no passado. Para isso, ela faz uso de um tempo verbal com o qual ainda não estamos familiarizados: o *Simple Past*.

Os verbos em inglês são classificados como *regulares* e *irregulares*. Essa classificação depende da maneira como o passado e o particípio passado são formados. Por exemplo, o verbo *work* é considerado regular, porque seu passado e seu particípio passado são formados com o acréscimo da partícula *ed*. Logo:

» Eu **trabalhei** = *I worked* (***worked*** = passado).
» Eu **tenho trabalhado** = *I have worked* (***worked*** = particípio passado, trabalhado).

Desse modo, ao estudarmos verbos no passado, em inglês, torna-se desnecessário memorizarmos os verbos regulares. Para isso, basta nos lembrarmos da adição da partícula *ed*. Vejamos um exemplo:

Simple Present

» I **work** every Saturday.

O vocábulo *every* nos dá a ideia de "ação habitual, rotineira"; consequentemente, usamos o *Simple Present*.

Simple Past

» I **worked** last Saturday.

O vocábulo *last* significa "passado"; se estamos nos referindo a uma ação que aconteceu no passado e deixamos claro quando essa ação ocorreu – *last Saturday* (sábado passado) –, devemos usar o *Simple Past*.

Já os verbos irregulares, como o próprio adjetivo *irregulares* sugere, não seguem regras. Portanto, precisam ser memorizados. Vejamos também um exemplo:

Simple Present

» Every day I **take** the children to school.

A frase expressa uma ação rotineira.

Simple Past

» Yesterday I **took** the children to school.

O vocábulo *yesterday*, que em português significa "ontem", explicita que a ação ocorreu no passado; por isso, usamos o *Simple Past*.

> Uma lista dos verbos irregulares está disponível nos apêndices, ao final deste livro.

Entretanto, é importante lembrar que, diferentemente do *Simple Present*, os verbos no passado não recebem a letra *s* na terceira pessoa do singular. Assim, devemos repetir o mesmo vocábulo em todas as pessoas, o que facilita bastante o seu uso. Por exemplo, o verbo *play* é regular; logo, deve ser conjugado do seguinte modo:

Chart 3.1 – Conjugation of the verb **to play**

Singular	Plural
I played	We played
You played	You played
He/She/It played	They played

Outro ponto que vale ressaltar é relativo à terminação dos verbos regulares. Os verbos regulares que terminam com a letra *y* precedida por uma consoante são expressos no passado com a substituição da letra *y* pela letra *i* e com o acréscimo da partícula *ed*. O verbo *study*, por exemplo, forma o passado da maneira mencionada (*study – studied*), como em:

» I **studied** English three weeks ago. (Eu estudei inglês há três semanas)

No que tange às formas interrogativa e negativa, no passado, usamos também o verbo auxiliar *do*, escrito como *did*, para a forma interrogativa, e *did not/didn't*, para a forma negativa. Como o verbo auxiliar (*did/did not*) já indica que nos referimos a uma ação acontecida no passado, o verbo principal volta para a forma básica, ou seja, o infinitivo. Observemos a conversa telefônica a seguir:

Jane: Hello, Jean. (1) **Did** you **have** a nice weekend?
Jean: (2) Yes, (3) **I did**. I **had** great fun in the weekend!!!
Jane: Really? What (4) **did** you **do**?
Jean: (5) I **visited** my best friend and (6) we **went** dancing at the new night club. (7) We **loved** it.
Jane: How wonderful! (8) **Did** your brother **go** with you?
Jean: (9) **No**, he **didn't**. (10) He **studied** all weekend, poor John.
Jane: Next time, call me! I feel like going together with you.
Jean: Sure! I have to hang up now. Someone is calling me. Bye!
Jane: Bye!

Exercises

3. Para verificar se você compreendeu como se formam os verbos no passado, leia o diálogo anterior novamente. Agora, insira os verbos destacados nas lacunas adequadas:

Verbo	Forma afirmativa	Forma interrogativa	Forma negativa
have		did you have	
do	did		

4. Na carta que Margareth escreveu para sua amiga Mary, foram usados cinco verbos (regulares e irregulares) no passado. Reescreva-os no quadro a seguir:

Verbo no infinitivo	Verbo no passado

Possessive adjectives

Agora releia a carta que Margareth e George escreveram para Mary e atente para os vocábulos em destaque. Como você pode perceber, são vocábulos relacionados à ideia de posse, por isso são denominados *adjetivos possessivos* (*possessive adjectives*). Todavia, há outro vocábulo destacado, que é o pronome possessivo *mine*. Façamos uma investigação mais pontual sobre o assunto:

	Possessive adjectives	Personal pronouns	Possessive pronouns
Chart 3.2 – Possessive adjectives and pronouns	my	I	mine
	your	you	yours
	his	he	his
	her	she	hers
	its	it	its
	our	we	ours
	your	you	yours
	their	they	theirs

50

Perceba que os pronomes pessoais foram inseridos entre os adjetivos e pronomes possessivos, porque sempre devemos combinar quaisquer dos possessivos, adjetivos e pronomes com os sujeitos, representados aqui pelos pronomes pessoais.

Veja os exemplos retirados da carta escrita por Margareth e George:

» (…) you don't have any plans for your Christmas holidays.
» Do you remember George had a terrible pain in the back? Well, his health is great now!
» My mother still has the problem in her feet.
» (…) we have plenty of time to stretch our legs.
» My parents live near here, so we can go to their house.

Para entender melhor o uso distinto de adjetivos possessivos e pronomes possessivos, é necessário observar o substantivo ao qual eles se referem. Em outras palavras, quando há um substantivo após o possessivo, usamos um adjetivo possessivo, que, lembramos, deve combinar com o sujeito da oração. Quando após o possessivo não há um substantivo, usamos o pronome possessivo. Veja o diálogo a seguir, em que Jennifer usa adjetivos e Mary usa pronomes possessivos:

» **Jennifer**: I like **my** manageress very much. She always talks to **her** staff in a very polite way.
» **Mary**: Really? Lucky you! **Mine** is a moody person and **his** – pointing to Peter – is a workaholic one.

Podemos notar que, ao falar de sua gerente, Jennifer opta pelos adjetivos possessivos, seguidos pelos substantivos adequados, uma vez que o assunto está sendo iniciado agora: *my manageress*, *her staff*. Já Mary opta por usar pronomes possessivos, uma vez que o assunto é o mesmo: a gerente da própria Mary e de Peter. Logo, não há necessidade de repetir o vocábulo *manageress*: *mine is a moody person/his is a workaholic one*. Certamente, as pessoas que estão conversando entendem que o assunto em pauta gira em torno das gerentes.

Exercises

5. Use the correct possessive adjective to complete the sentences:
   a) Peter goes to work on _____ bicycle.
   b) The manageress usually brings _____ lunch to work.
   c) I always do _____ job very carefully.
   d) Cars are useful. _____ prices are very high.
   e) We work with _____ parents.
   f) Do you really read _____ reports and e-mails?
   g) The staff clean _____ own office every Friday.
   h) The building entrance has _____ own telephone.

6. Answer the questions using possessive pronouns:

    My eyes are brown. What colour are yours?
      <u>Mine are brown.</u>

    a) My house is little. How about your friend Peter's house?
    _____

    b) My teacher is very patient. How about your sister's teacher?
    _____

    c) My car is not very comfortable. How about your parents' car?
    _____

    d) Your handwriting is not very nice. How about my handwriting?
    _____

    e) Do you think my explanation is clear?
    _____

EXPLORING vocabulary

Se observarmos mais uma vez a carta escrita por Margareth e George, encontraremos alguns vocábulos relacionados ao corpo humano, tais como *legs*, *feet*, *back* e *head*. Para melhor fixação desse conteúdo lexical, vamos examinar a imagem a seguir, que reproduz os corpos humanos masculino e feminino.

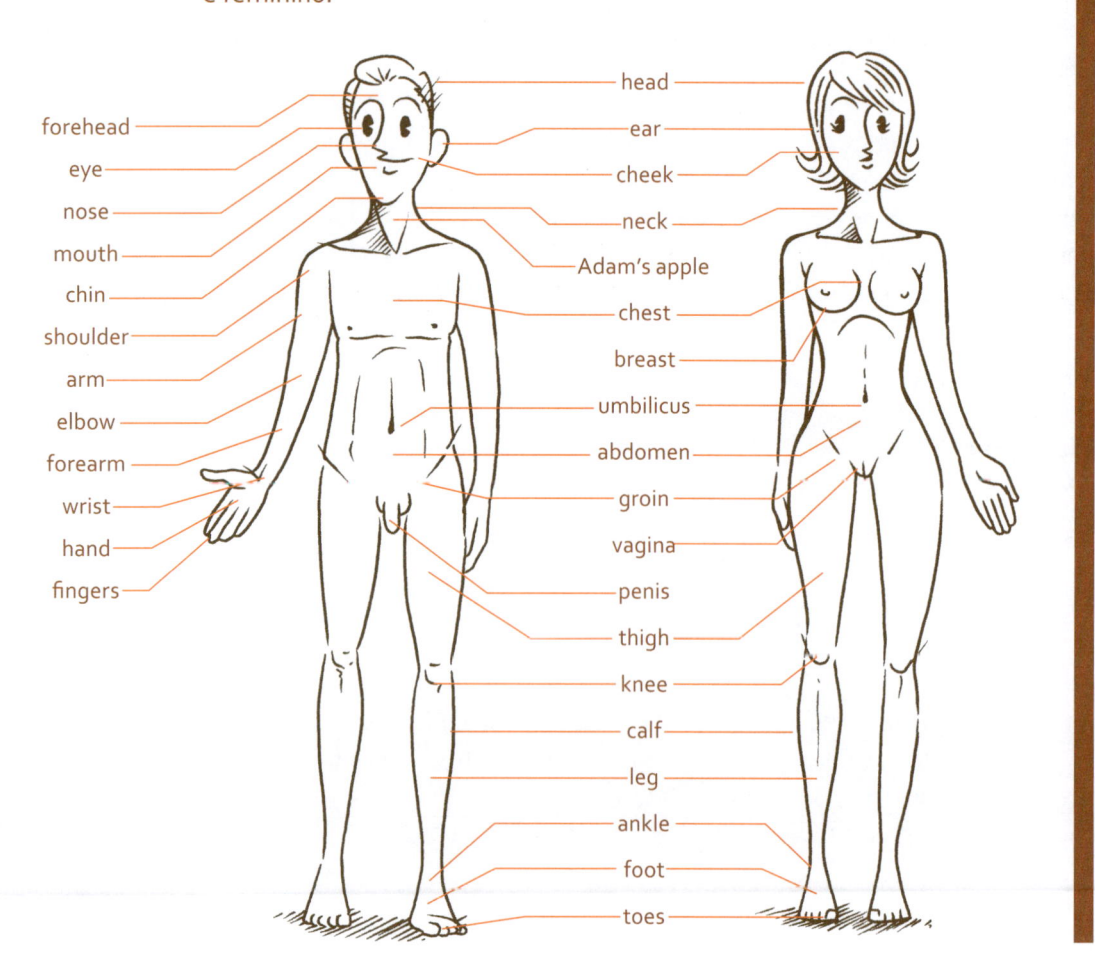

- forehead
- eye
- nose
- mouth
- chin
- shoulder
- arm
- elbow
- forearm
- wrist
- hand
- fingers
- head
- ear
- cheek
- neck
- Adam's apple
- chest
- breast
- umbilicus
- abdomen
- groin
- vagina
- penis
- thigh
- knee
- calf
- leg
- ankle
- foot
- toes

Lembramos que tais vocábulos são frequentemente relacionados a problemas de saúde. Em inglês, várias formas diferentes são usadas para se referir à dor, sendo possível que haja diferentes associações de vocábulos. Também usamos o vocábulo *ache* quando nos referir à dor de cabeça (*headache*), porém, em se tratando de dor na perna, optamos geralmente pelo vocábulo *pain* (*pain in the leg*). Para o verbo *doer*, podemos usar tanto *to hurt* quanto *to ache*.

Conforme mencionado anteriormente, denominamos essas associações lexicais de *lexical collocations*, ou seja, associações recorrentes de vocábulos. Vejamos alguns exemplos de associações relacionadas a problemas de saúde.

Quadro 3.3 – Associações relativas a problemas de saúde

Vocábulos associados a *ache*	Vocábulos associados a *pain*
Headache: dor de cabeça	*A pain in the arm*: dor no braço
Toothache: dor de dente	*A pain in the leg*: dor na perna
Stomachache: dor de estômago	*A pain in the neck*: dor no pescoço
Earache: dor de ouvido	*A pain in the knee*: dor no joelho
Backache: dor nas costas	*A pain in the elbow*: dor no cotovelo

Um outro ponto importante diz respeito aos adjetivos frequentemente usados perto dos substantivos *ache* e *pain*. Observe o diálogo a seguir:

Boss: What's the matter with you today?
Secretary: Sorry, but I have a terrible **headache**.
Boss: Why don't you take an aspirin?

O adjetivo *terrible* poderia ser substituído pelos vocábulos *bad*, *horrible* ou *awful*, que têm significado semelhante.

Prefixos e sufixos

Atualmente, o *e-mail* é a maneira mais eficiente e rápida para o envio de diferentes informações, o que contribui para a organização da empresa. Uma mensagem básica deve ser clara, concisa e direta para que possibilite uma boa comunicação entre o remetente e o receptor do *e-mail*. O entendimento de qualquer texto, inclusive de mensagens curtas em geral, está relacionado à gramática, ao estilo e, sobretudo, ao vocabulário adequado. Consequentemente, é importante prestar atenção especial na prefixação e na sufixação. Veja o exemplo a seguir:

```
Business dinner arrangements                                    _ | □ | x |
From:      Robert Jones
To:        Henry Smith
Date:      15 October 2009
Reference: Business dinner arrangements
```

Dear Mr. Smith,

I apologize for the first illegible list sent yesterday.

As required I am re-sending the attachment with the list of guests for the scheduled dinner on 23rd October. Thank you for your prompt attention to our booking arrangements. We appreciated it very much.

Yours sincerely,

Robert Jones

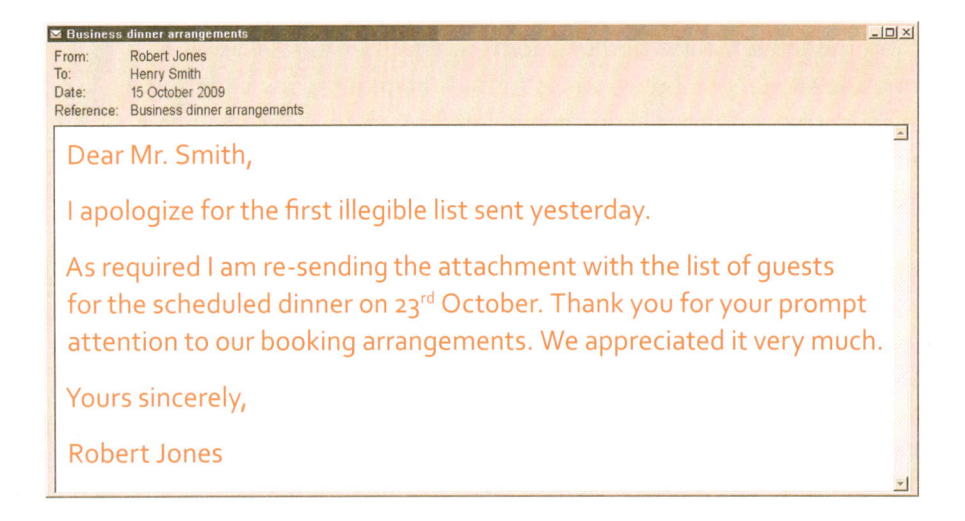

Nesse *e-mail*, podemos selecionar alguns vocábulos que foram formados com o acréscimo de prefixos e/ou sufixos. Por exemplo, o substantivo *business* foi formado pelo adjetivo *busy*, com o acréscimo do sufixo formador de substantivo *ness*. Isso significa que devemos nos lembrar de que os vocábulos terminados em *ness* são, geralmente, substantivos que foram formados a partir de um adjetivo.

Com relação aos prefixos, há, também, vocábulos formados por meio de prefixação, como o vocábulo *re-send*. Assim como na língua portuguesa, o prefixo *re* significa "novamente"; logo, o verbo *re-send* significa "enviar novamente", ou "reenviar".

Conforme mencionado anteriormente, é possível formar vocábulos com o acréscimo de prefixos e sufixos. No texto do *e-mail* apresentado como exemplo, podemos selecionar o vocábulo *illegible*. Em uma análise sobre formação de palavras, poderíamos perceber o seguinte:

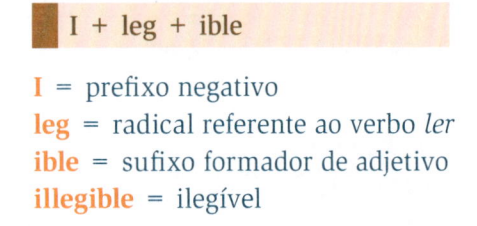

I + leg + ible

I = prefixo negativo
leg = radical referente ao verbo *ler*
ible = sufixo formador de adjetivo
illegible = ilegível

Agora, observemos outros prefixos e sufixos que poderiam ser úteis para nossa aquisição de vocabulário e a compreensão de texto.

Ao procurarmos palavras em um dicionário, devemos estar atentos para as palavras formadas por **prefixação** (acréscimo de um prefixo à palavra) e por **sufixação** (acréscimo de um sufixo à palavra).

Na maioria das palavras formadas por prefixação, precisamos separar o prefixo, deduzir o seu significado ou procurá-lo no dicionário, descobrir o significado do restante da palavra e, finalmente, entender a palavra completa.

- » **un** (prefixo) + **happy** (palavra primitiva) = **unhappy** (palavra derivada)
- » **dis** (prefixo) + **function** (palavra primitiva) = **disfunction** (palavra derivada)

O acréscimo do sufixo, geralmente, acarreta a mudança de classe gramatical do vocábulo. Desse modo, um adjetivo pode se tornar um advérbio, um verbo pode se tornar um substantivo, um substantivo pode se tornar um adjetivo e assim por diante.

- » **busy** (palavra primitiva) + **ness** (sufixo) = **business** (palavra derivada)
- » **treat** (palavra primitiva) + **ment** (sufixo) = **treatment** (palavra derivada)

Merecem uma atenção particular as terminações *ed* e *ing*, que, de acordo com o contexto, pertencem a diferentes classes gramaticais, como mostram os exemplos a seguir:

- » **Skimming** is a **reading** strategy. (substantivo/adjetivo)
- » The students are **reading** in the **reading** room. (verbo/adjetivo)
- » England is a **developed** country. (adjetivo)
- » Brasil **developed** a lot in the 70's. (verbo)

Chart 3.4 – Negative prefixes

Prefix	Meaning	Example
un- in- im- il- ir-	not	uncomfortable incomplete impossible illegal irregular, irrelevant
non-	not connected with; negative	non-smoking area
mis- mal-	bad, wrong	misunderstand malfunction
dis-	opposite feeling opposite action	disagree disconnect
anti-	against	antidemocratic
de-	reduce, reverse	decrease, decode
under-	too, little	underestimate

Chart 3.5 – Positive or negative prefixes

Prefix	Meaning	Example
re-	do again	reorganize
over-	too much	overload

Chart 3.6 – Prefixes of size

Prefix	Meaning	Example
semi-	half, partly	semiconductor
equi-	equal	equidistant

(continua)

(Chart 3.6 – conclusão)

Prefix	Meaning	Example
mini-	small	minicomputer
micro-	very small	microcomputer
macro-	large, great	macroeconomics
mega-		megabyte

Chart 3.7 – Prefixes of time and order

Prefix	Meaning	Example
ante-	before	antecedent
pre-		predecessor
prime-	first	primary, primitive
post-	after	postdated postpone
retro-	backward	retroactive

Chart 3.8 – Prefixes of location

Prefix	Meaning	Example
inter-	between, among	interface, interactive
super-	over	supersonic
trans-	across	transmit, transfer
in-	in	include, intrinsic
ex-	out	exclude, extrinsic
extra-	beyond	extraordinary
sub-	under	subschema
infra-	below	infra-red
peri-	around half, partly	peripheral

Agora vejamos alguns sufixos (*suffixes*):

Chart 3.9 – Suffixes that form nouns (noun-forming suffixes)

Suffix	Meaning	Example
-ant		assistant
-ar	people who do things	liar, beggar
-er		teacher
-ent		president
-er		programmer
-ian	a verb + a suffix = noun	electrician
-ist	(people)	analyst, typist
-or		operator

Chart 3.10 – Suffixes that form nouns from verbs

Suffix	Meaning	Example
-ance -ence	act of, condition of	performance, acceptance, existence
-ery	act of, art of, occupation	discovery, robbery
-ion -tion	the act of, condition of the act of, condition of	compilation, conversion, attention information
-ment	result of / act of, condition, state of being	development, measurement, disappointment
-ing	activity of/ quality of	reading, fishing

Chart 3.11 – Suffixes that form nouns from adjectives

Suffix	Meaning	Example
-ance, -ence	quality, condition, state	abundance, absence, independence
-ancy, -ency, -cy	state / quality	constancy, hesitancy, consistency frequency
-ity, -ety	quality or state of being	electricity, reality, activity, anxiety
-ness	quality or state of being	illness, kindness, darkness

Chart 3.12 – Suffixes that form nouns from nouns

Suffix	Meaning	Example
-cy	domain or condition	pharmacy, presidency, lunacy
-dom	state of being	freedom
-hood	members of a group	motherhood, boyhood, priesthood, brotherhood
-ism	act or result of condition/state – theory, belief	terrorism, organism, magnetism, heroism, nationalism, realism
-ship	state or quality of / art or skill	friendship, relationship, partnership, leadership

Agora vejamos sufixos que formam advérbios:

Chart 3.13 – Suffixes that form adverbs (adverb-forming suffixes)

Suffix	Meaning	Examples
adjective + ly	in a certain way, in the manner of	electronically, logically
noun + ly	each, every like, similarity	weekly, yearly manly, monthly

A seguir, alguns sufixos que formam verbos:

Chart 3.14 – Suffixes that form verbs (verb-forming suffixes) from nouns

Suffix	Meaning	Examples
-ize/-ise	to make into or like become to act in a certain way treat	humanize crystallize theorize, sympathize, criticize
-en	gain, cause to have	strengthen, lengthen
-ify	make, form into, cause to become	simplify, classify, solidify

Chart 3.15 – Suffixes that form verbs from adjectives

Suffix	Meaning	Examples
-ate	become or cause to become	automate, activate, calculate
-en	make or become	harden, widen, deepen

Por último, vejamos sufixos que formam adjetivos:

Chart 3.16 – Suffixes that form adjectives (adjective-forming suffixes)

Suffix	Meaning	Examples
-ful	full of, having the quality of, tending to be	beautiful, careful, harmful
-less	free from, without, unable to do or to be	careless, fearless, homeless, countless, helpless
-ous	the person or thing has, is full of, or is like	ambitious, anxious, glorious
-ish	having the quality, like, color	foolish, girlish, yellowish
-al -ar -ic/-ical	having the quality of	computational, logical, circular, automatic, economical
-ate	having the quality of	affectionate
-en	made of, like	golden, wooden

Chart 3.17 – Suffixes that form adjectives from verbs

Suffix	Meaning	Examples
-able -ible	capable of being, able to be	comparable, divisible
-ive	capable of being or doing	interactive, attractive
-ent -ed -ing	being or acting in a certain way, having the quality	sufficient, the computed idea, running shoes

Verbo *to be*: in the past

Neste capítulo, abordamos os verbos regulares e irregulares e o passado desses verbos. Todavia, é necessário que destaquemos o *Simple Past* do verbo *to be* (*ser/estar*, em português), cuja conjugação pode ser mais bem visualizada no quadro a seguir:

Chart 3.18 – Verb *to be*

Affirmative form	Interrogative	Negative
I was	Was I?	I was not/wasn't.
You were	Were you?	You were not/weren't.
He was	Was he?	He was not/wasn't.
She was	Was she?	She was not/wasn't.
It was	Was it?	It was not/wasn't.
We were	Were we?	We were not/weren't.
You were	Were you?	You were not/weren't.
They were	Were they?	They were not/weren't.

É necessário dar certo destaque a esse verbo por ser bastante diferente dos outros verbos em relação à forma no passado. Além disso, o passado do verbo *to be* é utilizado para formar alguns novos verbos, como o verbo *nascer* (*to be born*). Assim, eu nasci = *I was born*, como na música do grupo musical Queen, *I was born to love you*. Outro exemplo é a música

Born in the USA, de Bruce Springsteen, que é um símbolo do orgulho de ter nascido nos EUA.

Exercise

7. Let's use the past of the verb *to be* to answer the questions below:
   a) Where were you born?

   b) When were you born?

   c) How are most babies born in Brazil nowadays – cesarean or normal birth?

   d) Where were you yesterday morning, at home, at work or anywhere else?

   e) Who were you with in your last vacation?

A LITTLE BIT OF READING

Business meetings

The most important thing to remember when making appointments is that you are in a formal situation; therefore, do not talk too much. You can expand on what you have to offer when you get to the appointment.
Remember the following points:

» What you need is your opening statement (something you know about them or a referral).
» You need to have also an "interest–grabbing" sentence, something that offers the customer a major benefit.

> » Remember to request the appointment ensuring you give options of days and hours, so the prospect cannot simply say "yes" or "no".
>
> Here are some useful expressions to be used when making appointments:
>
> I'd like to make an appointment with...
> Could we meet to discuss...
> What day will be convenient for you?
> What time would be more suitable?
> How about...?
> I'll look forward to seeing you.

Exercises Approaching Collocations

8. Agora, escolha o melhor título para esse texto:
   a) The best time to make appointments.
   b) What to talk about during appointments.
   c) How to say "no" in an appointment.
   d) How to make an appointment.
   e) How to dress in a business appointment.

9. Answer the questions below choosing one or more words that collocate to the one in the question.

   For example:

   What may you have?
   (x) a meal
   (x) a drink
   ( ) a museum
   ( ) 20 years old
   (x) health problems

   It is possible to have a meal, to have a drink and to have health problems, but it is certainly not possible to have a museum or have 20 years old.

   a) What may you look forward to?
      ( ) an early reply
      ( ) seeing someone
      ( ) going abroad
      ( ) having a terrible headache
      ( ) reading an illegible e-mail

   b) What may you hang up?
      ( ) a book
      ( ) the door
      ( ) the phone

( ) the office
( ) the dinner

c) How may a boss be?
( ) comfortable
( ) workaholic
( ) bossy
( ) demanding
( ) hard-working

d) How may people dress?
( ) intensively
( ) smartly
( ) greatly
( ) absolutely
( ) casually

Síntese do capítulo

Neste capítulo, lidamos com várias questões importantes para o nosso aprendizado de língua inglesa. Primeiramente, abordamos o tempo verbal *Simple Past* em suas formas afirmativa, interrogativa e negativa, bem como adjetivos e pronomes possessivos. No que concerne à leitura e à compreensão de textos, tratamos da escrita de cartas informais e de mensagens em *e-mails*. No que tange ao léxico, além de formação de palavras, vimos também os vocábulos referentes ao corpo humano e à dor física.

Meios de transporte 4

Nos dias de hoje, um dos aspectos mais importantes na vida das pessoas são os meios de transporte, não só aqueles que usamos para nos locomovermos diariamente, mas também aqueles que nos cercam e que, muitas vezes, afetam nossa saúde. No mundo todo, as pessoas são incentivadas a andar a pé e de bicicleta ou a usar o transporte público, mas, ainda assim, o uso de carros na vida urbana tornou-se rotina. Além disso, a movimentação de pessoas entre cidades e países aumentou, sendo muito comum, atualmente, viajar de ônibus, de avião, ou até mesmo de trem – um dos meios de transporte mais populares na Europa.

Leia, a seguir, um texto sobre as escolhas de transporte nas cidades e responda algumas perguntas na sequência.

A LITTLE BIT OF READING

Urban transportation choices

Do we want an auto-city or an eco-city? A city for cars or a city for people?

Transportation determines urban form, and will determine how we conduct daily life. Do we really need a car or can we walk or cycle?

Car use is NOT inevitable; it is only *one way out of many* to move around. We can make different choices and set different mobility priorities that produce different results for daily life and economic development.

If our option is to use cars, then our choice is to build a more sprawling city so we can have space for them. If we give priority for biking and walking, we will be able to build a compact city which is for people's use.

Urban quality of life, aesthetics and economic development is handicapped by reliance on the automobile. Rethinking mobility opens the possibility of transforming any city into a people-oriented, economically competitive, sustainable urban oasis. In the short term it will be more livable and marketable. In the long term it will remain resilient in the face of energy descent.

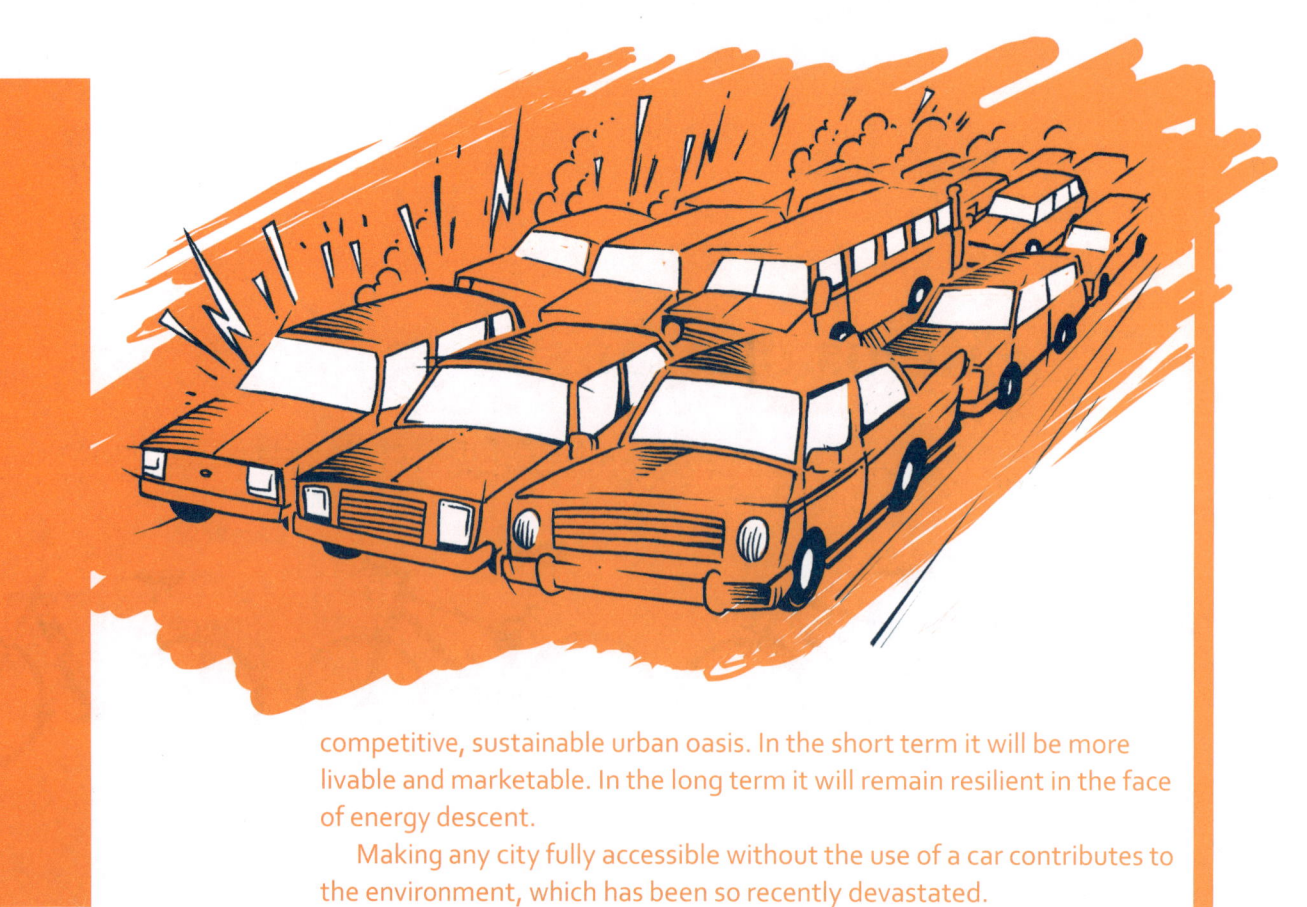

Making any city fully accessible without the use of a car contributes to the environment, which has been so recently devastated.

Source: Adapted from Morache, 2005.

Exercise

1. Answer the questions below:

   a) Which would you prefer, an auto-city or an eco-city?
   _____

   b) What happens to urban quality of life using cars?
   _____

   c) What is your mode of transportation to go to and from school, work?
   _____

A LITTLE BIT OF READING

London Underground

According to the Mayor's[1] statement, London's transport system should facilitate access to opportunities for all its people and enterprises in a very efficient way.

Here are some facts and figures:

---

[1] Boris Johnson has set out his vision for transport in London over the next 20 years with the Mayor's Transport Strategy.

- » Number of km travelled by each tube train each year: 123,600 km.
- » Total number of passengers carried each year: 1,065 million.
- » Number of individual passengers carried on the tube each year: 28 million.
- » Average train speed: 33 km per hour.
- » Length of network: 402 km.
- » Proportion of the network that is in tunnels: 45 per cent.
- » Longest continuous tunnel: East Finchley to Morden (via Bank), 27.8 km.
- » Total number of escalators: 422.
- » Longest escalator: Angel. 60 m (with a vertical rise of 27.5 m).
- » Price of a single Underground ticket bought in London: £4.00.
- » Busiest stations: during the three-hour morning peak, London's busiest tube station is Waterloo, with 49,000 people entering. The busiest station in terms of passengers each year is Victoria, with 77 million.
- » The Underground name first appeared on stations in 1908.
- » London Underground has been known as 'The Tube' since 1890, when the first deep-level electric railway line was opened.
- » The Tube's world-famous logo, 'The Roundel' (a red circle crossed by a horizontal blue bar), first appeared in 1908.

Source: Adapted from TFL, 1011.

Pronomes interrogativos iniciados com *how*

Como vimos no início do Capítulo 2, as *wh question words* (*what*, *where*, *when*, *which*, *why*, *whose*, *who*, *how*) são usadas para fazer perguntas. Veremos agora que, adicionando outras palavras a *how*, podemos modificar o sentido desse pronome e ampliar o vocabulário, construindo, assim, termos que podem ser usados em outras frases interrogativas.

Exercises

2. Com base no texto que vimos na seção anterior, que trata sobre o metrô de Londres, responda às seguintes perguntas:
   a) How long (*há quanto tempo*) ago did the Underground name appear on the stations?
   _____

   b) How long (*qual o comprimento*) is the London Underground?
   _____

c) How old (*quantos anos*) are you?
_____

d) How far (*que distância*) is it from East Finchley to Morden?
_____

e) How high (*que altura*) is the longest escalator?
_____

f) How tall (*que altura*) are you?
_____

g) How big (*que tamanho*) is your company?
_____

h) How often (*com que frequência*) do you take vacations?
_____

i) How many (*quantos*) passengers travel on the London Underground each year?
_____

j) How much (*quanto*) does a single Underground ticket bought in London cost?
_____

k) How soon (*em quanto tempo*) can you finish the report?
_____

3. A seguir, complete as frases utilizando os pronomes interrogativos que aparecem nas questões do exercício 2:
   a) _____ did the meeting last?
      About 1 hour.
   b) _____ money did they invest in the new company?
      We don't know.
   c) _____ does your boss travel on business?
      Usually once a month.
   d) _____ is the new company building?
      I think it will have about 30 floors.
   e) _____ is the new building from the old one?
      About 10 km.
   f) _____ employees does your company have?
      About 300 employees.
   g) _____ did the new computers cost?
      About $950.00 each.
   h) _____ is the new director?
      He's very tall. I think he's over 1.90 m.
   i) _____ is the training program?
      About three months.

j) _____ is the new supervisor?
   He looks so young. Oh, he's in his thirties.
k) _____ is the new parking lot?
   It's big enough for about 100 cars.

Substantivos e advérbios contáveis e incontáveis

Assim como na língua portuguesa, no inglês também encontramos substantivos e advérbios que não são contáveis, ou seja, palavras que não podem ser colocadas no plural. Observe alguns exemplos:

Materials (gold, iron, silver, paper etc.) are uncountable:

» Example: **Wood** burns easily.

Food (cheese, butter, meat, salt, pepper, bacon, sugar, bread, chocolate, honey, jam etc.) is generally uncountable:

» Example: We need to buy **rice**.

Liquids (coffee, milk, water, tea, lemonade, petrol, oil etc.) are uncountable:

» Example: Let's have some **wine**.

Abstract nouns (beauty, happiness, friendship etc.) are uncountable:
» Example: **Love** is a many splendor thing.

Others (hair, snow, furniture, weather, advice, information etc.):
» Example: It's good to earn **money**.

Some uncountable nouns in English are countable nouns in Portuguese, like: *advice, baggage, luggage, information, bread, permission* etc. There are others that are written in the plural but are also uncountable: *news, glasses, scissors* etc.

For uncountable and countable plural we use *some*, not *a/an*:
- » They have to buy **some bread**.
- » We need **some pens and pencils**.

Exercise

4. Choose the best alternative to complete the sentences.
   a) Let's have a fire. Can you go and get _____.
      ( ) a wood
      ( ) some wood
   b) Can you lend me _____.
      ( ) some money
      ( ) a few money
   c) My friend needs _____.
      ( ) some advice
      ( ) an advice
   d) When _____ on? I haven't heard any today.
      ( ) are the news
      ( ) is the news
   e) The assembly line was full of _____.
      ( ) a noise
      ( ) noise
   f) I want to write a letter. I need _____.
      ( ) some writing paper
      ( ) a writing paper
   g) Can we help you out with the _____?
      ( ) luggage
      ( ) luggages
   h) They bought a new house and some new _____.
      ( ) furniture
      ( ) furnitures
   i) I'm going out. Would you like some _____?
      ( ) bread
      ( ) breads
   j) For this job it is necessary lots of _____.
      ( ) experiences
      ( ) experience

A LITTLE BIT OF READING

Transportation

Today, people use different means of transportation in different parts of the world, as it varies depending on which country the executive is traveling to.

Transportation, **itself**, around the world, changes in types according to the culture of each country involved. Let's check some unusual types:

In India, for example, the people, **themselves**, use *hand-pulled rickshaws*, a two-wheeled cart where one or two people sit and are pulled by the person, **himself**, to go around in small cities. It has been banned, but it is still found in some parts of the country. The *cycle rickshaw* is also found, which is bigger than a tricycle where two people sit on an elevated seat at the back and a person pedals from the front. It is a non-polluting and inexpensive mean of transport.

In China, we still think of thousands of people using the bicycle for transportation. Even though this is still true, there has been a major growth on all means of transportation in China. We find electric bicycles, bus rapid transit, trolley bus and tramway systems, besides the automobiles, airplanes and trains. The rail system, **itself**, is the major transportation in China, and it is one of the largest in the world.

So, as we can see, travelers should be aware of all these different types and verify which one will be more convenient for a specific trip. Of course, in every country, including the two mentioned above, it is possible to make plane and car reservations, which are the most common ones around the world.

4 • Meios de transporte

A LITTLE BIT OF GRAMMAR

Reflexive pronouns

Como vimos no texto, algumas palavras foram destacadas. Essas palavras são denominadas *reflexive pronouns*. Esses pronomes são usados quando o sujeito e o objeto da frase são os mesmos, como em:

» **Tom** cut **himself** while he was shaving. (Tom cortou-se enquanto se barbeava)

Também podemos usá-los para dar ênfase ao sujeito:

» It's best if you do it **yourself**. (É melhor se você mesmo o fizer)

Os pronomes reflexivos são os seguintes:

Chart 4.1 – Pronomes reflexivos

Singular		Plural	
I	Myself	We	Ourselves
You	Yourself	You	Yourselves
He She It	Himself Herself itself	They	Themselves

Exercícios

5. Copie os pronomes reflexivos do texto "Transportation" e escreva a que substantivos eles se referem:
   a) _____ – _____
   b) _____ – _____
   c) _____ – _____
   d) _____ – _____

6. Complete with the correct interrogative pronoun:
   a) _____ is his full name? It's John Brown.
   b) _____ is the new software? We don't have the prices yet.
   c) _____ are you going on vacation? Maybe to Australia.
   d) _____ did you work in this company? For about three years.
   e) _____ secretaries are there in the department? About four.
   f) _____ do you have general meetings? Once every two weeks.
   g) _____ is the company going to start hiring again? Probably next month.
   h) _____ from downtown is the new building? About ten miles.
   i) _____ are they going to meet in Europe? Because it's more convenient for everyone.

7. Mark the sentences correct (C) or incorrect (I) and choose the alternative with the correct order:
   ( ) The informations from the newspapers are not always reliable.
   ( ) The news are usually very depressing.
   ( ) They didn't have much luggage during the trip.
   ( ) We need to buy some paper for the office.
   ( ) She is always asking for advices.

   a) I, I, C, C, C.
   b) I, I, C, C, I.
   c) C, I, C, C, C.
   d) I, I, I, C, C.
   e) C, I, I, C, C.

8. Complete the following sentences with a reflexive pronoun:
   a) Mary, _____, likes to check the reports.
   b) John and Peter locked _____ out of the house.
   c) I'm trying to do it _____, so I can learn well.
   d) Don't worry about us. We can take care of _____.
   e) It's not difficult. I'm sure you can do it _____.

Curiosidades

Geralmente, na língua inglesa, os pronomes não são escritos no plural. A exceção são os pronomes reflexivos. Como vimos, no singular escrevemos *self* (*myself*) e no plural *selves* (*ourselves*). Um exemplo pertinente são as expressões *sirva-se* e *sirvam-se*, que em inglês são, respectivamente, *help yourself* e *help yourselves*.

Plural

Na maior parte das vezes, para colocar um termo no plural, basta acrescentar a letra *s* (*book = books*). Em palavras que apresentam terminações em *sh, ch, s, ss, z, o, x*, acrescentam-se as letras *es*.

- » match – match**es**
- » wash – wash**es**
- » bus – bus**es**
- » miss – miss**es**
- » box – box**es**
- » potato – potato**es**

Outras palavras apresentam plural irregular. A seguir, destacamos alguns dos mais comuns.

Chart 4.2 – Substantivos com plural irregular

Singular	Plural	Singular	Plural
mouse	mice	self	selves
child	children	shelf	shelves
foot	feet	thief	thieves
man	men	wife	wives
woman	women	scarf	scarves / scarfs
tooth	teeth	knife	knives
person	people	ox	oxen
half	halves	sheep	sheep
goose	geese	deer	deer
leaf	leaves	radio	radios
life	lives	piano	pianos
loaf	loaves	photo	photos

Existem outras palavras que só usamos no plural e algumas que terminam em *s*, mas que, geralmente, não representam o plural.

» **Gymnastics** is my favorite sport.

Há também outro grupo de palavras que, aparentemente, estão no singular, mas que sempre são usadas com o verbo no plural.

» The company **staff** work overtime on Mondays.

Ainda há mais outro grupo de palavras que podem estar tanto no singular quanto no plural.

» This is a rare **species** of birds. There are many species of birds.

Para melhor visualização, observe os exemplos do quadro a seguir:

Chart 4.3 – Representação do plural em grupos diferentes de palavras

Vocábulos que só usamos no plural	Vocábulos que terminam em *s*, mas estão no singular	Vocábulos que não terminam em *s*, mas estão no plural	Vocábulos que podem estar no plural ou no singular
shorts jeans slacks pajamas scissors glasses	economics mathematics physics economics athletics news	police staff people	means species series

Não podemos deixar de mostrar que existe outra regra para a formação do plural: as palavras que terminam em *y* e são precedidas por consoante perdem o *y* e recebem em seu lugar *ies*, como nos exemplos a seguir:

» city – cit**ies**
» copy – cop**ies**
» party – part**ies**
» baby – bab**ies**
» country – countr**ies**
» family – famil**ies**

» lady – lad**ies**
» secretary – secretar**ies**

Exercise Approaching Collocations

9. Choose a word from the box to complete the sentences:

system | hire | rent | speed | single or a return
trip | on vacation | rush | stuck | reservation

a) I would like to make a _____ for an ensuite room for tomorrow, please.
b) As the secretary was dismissed last week, we are going to _____ a new one this month.
c) When I travel abroad, it is always very useful to _____ a car, so we can go everywhere we want.
d) Going _____ is always a great pleasure, especially when the weather is fine.
e) London has an efficient transportation _____, so there is not so much traffic jam, fortunately.
f) I am not sure if I am going to return tomorrow, so I don't know if I should buy a _____ ticket.
g) In the USA, people prefer to use the expression round _____ for when the meaning is going and returning anywhere.
h) In São Paulo, at the _____ hour, people generally spend long hours stuck in the traffic jam.
i) What is the _____ limit in the highways in the USA, do you know?
j) It is terrible to get _____ in a traffic jam after a long day work.

Síntese do capítulo

Neste capítulo, abordamos os meios de transporte e a importância de estarmos atualizados em relação aos costumes de outros países, pois, muitas vezes, é necessário que nos adaptemos a outros tipos de locomoção e ao respectivo vocabulário.

Em relação à parte estrutural, trabalhamos com: pronomes interrogativos iniciados com *how*; substantivos e advérbios contáveis e não contáveis; e pronomes reflexivos. Verificamos também como são formados o plural regular e irregular dos vocábulos, bem como algumas regras especiais.

A fim de trabalhar os aspectos lexicais do capítulo, foram apresentados dois textos e um diálogo, que trataram de aspectos relacionados às diferentes culturas de outros países em relação aos diversos meios de transporte.

As leituras propostas pretendem ser pertinentes ao que foi trabalhado neste capítulo, proporcionando a você oportunidades de aumentar seu vocabulário e conhecer outras culturas.

Vestuário adequado para o ambiente de trabalho

5

Embora o vestuário profissional possa, à primeira vista, parecer um tema supérfluo, acreditamos que se preocupar com a aparência no local de trabalho é extremamente necessário, especialmente em se tratando de *business*.

A LITTLE BIT OF READING

Work dress codes and image collection

A work dress code is a set of standards that companies develop to help provide their employees with guidance about what is appropriate to wear to work. Work dress codes range from formal to business casual to casual. The formality of the workplace dress code is normally determined by the amount of interaction employees have with customers at their work location. These sample work dress codes include business casual, business casual for manufacturing, casual, and formal work dress codes (Heathfield, 2012).

Exercise

1. Read the text and complete the chart (the 'X' means there is no word for that category):

Noun	Verb	Adjective	Adverb
collection		X	X
employee			X
guidance		X	X
business	X		
formality	X		
interaction		X	X
normality	X		

Sabemos que, no mundo corporativo, a sexta-feira, diferentemente dos outros dias, é o dia de usar *casual clothes*. Então, vamos resolver o que vestir na próxima sexta-feira e impressionar com nossa escolha?

A LITTLE BIT OF READING

How to dress to impress on Casual Fridays

Casual Fridays can be fun and are popular with employees. However, they can also be tricky, especially for new employees. Women may have an especially hard time determining the line between business casual and unprofessional. Casual Fridays are a chance for you to show you're fun and a team player but that you still take your job seriously. Here you will learn a few tips for dressing to impress on Casual Friday.

Have a look at Mr. Gray's commentary for next Friday:

I am going to wear a polo shirt (also known as golf shirts, which come in a variety of colors), and a pair of khaki pants. This is the way I feel really comfortable without being inconvenient, as it is a work place. However, it is a good idea to bring a change of clothes in your car, in case I get called to meet a client or attend a business meeting.

On the other hand, let's see Mrs. Johnson's choice for next Friday:

I think people should always try to stay professional even if it's casual Friday, so **I am going to wear** a sweater set and pants. In my opinion, this is a great outfit for women to stay stylish on a casual Friday. I can also choose a casual skirt, but certainly **I am not going to wear** anything shorter than an inch above the knee. As for shoes, I am going to wear either flat or low-heel shoes, which are also appropriate.

What about you? **What are you going to wear** next Casual Friday?

Source: Adapted from Rigg, 2012.

5 • Vestuário adequado para o ambiente de trabalho

Exercise

2. No texto acima, os verbos destacados estão em que tempo?
   a) Present.
   b) Past.
   c) Future.

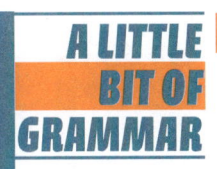

A LITTLE BIT OF GRAMMAR

Futuro

Como podemos observar, os verbos destacados estão no futuro, uma vez que as opiniões são sobre o que vestir na próxima sexta-feira. Entretanto, notamos o uso de dois tipos de futuro, o *Going to Future* e o *Will Future*. Vejamos a diferença entre os dois.

Going to Future

■ Sujeito + verbo to be + going to + verbo principal

As formas interrogativa e negativa são formadas do mesmo modo como fazemos normalmente com o verbo *to be*, ou seja, usamos a inversão entre o sujeito e o verbo *to be* para a forma interrogativa e introduzimos a partícula negativa *not* para a forma negativa.

No texto "How to dress to impress on Casual Fridays", há exemplos interessantes. Vamos selecionar alguns:

» I **am going to wear** a sweater set.

» I **am not going to wear** anything shorter than an inch above the knee.

» What **are you going to wear**?

É importante destacar que, no texto que acabamos de ler, o *Going to Future* sugere que a roupa para o *Casual Friday* já havia sido escolhida.

Will Future

■ Sujeito + will ('ll) + verbo

A forma interrogativa é formada pela inversão entre o sujeito e a partícula *will*. Já a forma negativa é formada com a introdução da partícula de negação *not* após o vocábulo *will* (*will not* ou *won't*), como neste exemplo, em que a recepcionista, Karen, resolve o que vai vestir e fala:

» **Karen**: Well, a suit is a nice idea. Yes! I have just decided: **I will wear** a red dress. I was thinking about wearing jeans but I won't.

Nesse exemplo, uma vez que o verbo em questão é o mesmo (*to wear*), não há necessidade de repeti-lo na sentença negativa.

Vale ressaltar que usamos o *Will Future* quando decidimos o que faremos no momento da fala, ou seja, diferentemente do *Going to Future,* não há planejamento anterior.

Outro ponto relevante é relativo ao uso de *will* em outras situações, especialmente para pedirmos alguma coisa. Nesse caso, é muito comum a expressão *Will you please...?*, usada comumente na forma interrogativa como um sinônimo de *Can you please...?*

» **Boss**: It's getting cold. **Will you please close** the window, Jane?
» **Jane**: Sure! I'll do it.

Exercises

3. Make sentences in the Future using *will* or *won't*. Give your opinion doing the following dialogue:

   A: When will someone discover a cure for Aids?

   B: I don't know, maybe in about two or three years' time.

   A: I hope so.

   a) who / win the next World Cup?
   _____
   _____
   _____

   b) who / the next president / be?
   _____
   _____
   _____

   c) what / next year's fashion / be like?
   _____
   _____
   _____

   d) where / you / be in ten years?
   _____
   _____
   _____

4. Make sentences starting with *when* or *as soon as*:

   I / get home / go straight to bed.
   When I get home, I will go straight to bed.

   a) he arrives / I / phone you.
      As soon as _____
   b) We / decide about the job / we / let you know.
      As soon as _____
   c) You / see Malcolm / you / not / recognize him.
      When _____
   d) I / pass my driving test / I / buy / car.
      As soon as _____

5. Make three affirmative and three negative sentences about your plans for next Sunday, choosing the expressions from the box. Follow the pattern using the *Going to Future*:

   Next Sunday, I am going to get up late, but my children are going to get up early because they are going to chat on the internet.

   get up late get up early go for a walk go for a drive visit my parents
   visit my friends watch TV study for the test read the newspaper
   write e-mails chat on the Internet cook have lunch at a restaurant
   eat Italian food have a pizza for dinner go to bed late
   go to the cinema go to church meet friends

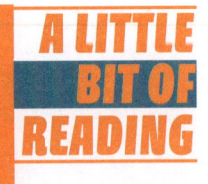

   _____
   _____
   _____
   _____
   _____
   _____

A LITTLE BIT OF READING

Negotiating

Negotiating is a skill that **may** be developed and used in a variety of situations. When you were children, you negotiated with your parents over all kinds of things. As you grew **older**, the nature and complexity of your negotiation changed. Consequently, some people are **better** at negotiating than others. In fact, it is very **difficult** to say who is the **best** negotiator, because negotiating is an art and an art cannot be measured.

Some negotiations **may** last a few minutes and others **may** last for decades, so have a look at these examples of negotiation:

» Some people pay $10,000 **less** than others for automobiles because they got prepared, were informed and negotiated effectively, so people shoud get prepared and well-informed before they start negotiating.
» The service you receive in a restaurant is, in effect, a negotiation for a **fair** tip, so, as everybody knows, the waiter **might** or **might not** get some extra money, depending on how he treats the customers.

Preparation is the key!

I think people **should** simulate when they go through a negotiating situation. For example, when you **need** to meet a superior, you imagine what you will talk about and prepare your responses mentally.

Qualities of a good negotiator

He/she should:
» Be prepared.
» Know his/ her goals.
» Set limits.
» Learn from sources (such as politicians, movies, diplomats, soap operas etc.).
» Know when to stop talking and close the deal.

Exercise

6. In the passage above, there are several adjectives and adverbs which are highlighted. Let's match them to their opposite meaning:

a) older   ( ) inferior
b) better   ( ) uninformed
c) difficult   ( ) ineffectively
d) less   ( ) unprepared
e) informed   ( ) worse
f) effectively   ( ) badly-informed
g) prepared   ( ) unfair
h) well-informed ( ) younger, newer
i) fair   ( ) easy
j) superior   ( ) more

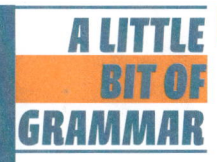

A LITTLE BIT OF GRAMMAR

Comparisons

In communication we use a lot of positive and negative adjectives. In fact, we use adjectives in several situations, but mainly when we describe and compare people, animals, objects etc. Let's see how we make comparisons in English.

Grau dos adjetivos[1]

Comparatives

There are three types of comparatives:

1. When someone or something is the same as the other.

   » A&C factory is 30 years old and V&X factory is 30 years old too, so A&C is **as old as** V&X.
   » The Smith Accounting Firm has 200 customers and The Johnson Insurance Firm has 200 customers too, so there are **as many** customers in one firm **as** in the other.

   To make a sentence in the comparative of equality we use:

   > as or so + adjective or adverb + as

2. When someone or something is less than the other.

   » Cars are generally expensive. I paid $1200,00 for a Fiat and $12.000,00 for a BMW.
   » So a Fiat is **less expensive than** a BMW.

   To make a sentence in the comparative of inferiority we use:

   > less + adjective + than

3. When someone or something is more than the other, we have two choices.

   » Cars are generally expensive. I paid $1200,00 for a Fiat and $12.000,00 for a BMW. So a BMW is **more expensive than** a Fiat.

   To make a sentence in the comparative of superiority, if the adjective is long (that is, has more than two syllables), we use:

   > more + adjective + than

   » Peter is tall. He is 1.85 m. Paul is tall too. He is 1.95 m. So Paul is **taller than** Peter.

   To make a sentence in the comparative of superiority, if the adjective is short, that is, has less than 2 syllables, we use:

   > adjective + er + than

---

[1] Visando à ampliação do seu vocabulário, as explicações sobre grau dos adjetivos serão apresentadas em inglês.

Superlatives

There are two types of superlatives:

4. When something or someone is **the least** of all, we use the superlative of inferiority.

» All the hotels near the airport are comfortable, but in PH Hotel rooms do not have air conditioning. So PH Hotel is **the least comfortable** hotel near the airport.

To make a sentence in the superlative of inferiority we use:

| the least + adjective

5. When something or someone is **the most** of all, we use the superlative of superiority and, for that, we have two choices. For example:

» All the secretaries in the company are efficient but nobody is like Mary. So Mary is **the most efficient** secretary in the company.

To make a sentence in the superlative of superiority, if the adjective is long, that is, if it has more than two syllables, we use:

| the most + adjective

But, now, look at this second example:

» Many cities in Brazil are cold, but no city is as cold as São Joaquim, in Santa Catarina; so São Joaquim, in Santa Catarina, is **the coldest** city in Brasil.

To make a sentence in the superlative of superiority, if the adjective is short, that is, if it has less than two syllables, we use:

| the + adjective + est

To help you understand better, take a look at the examples in the following charts:

Chart 5.2 – Adjectives with one syllable

Adjectives	Comparative	Superlative
old	older than	the oldest
tall	taller than	the tallest
cheap	cheaper than	the cheapest
late	later than	the latest
new	newer than	the newest
long	longer than	the longest
short	shorter than	the shortest
fat	fatter than	the fattest
big	bigger than	the biggest
hot	hotter than	the hottest
cold	colder than	the coldest
dark	darker than	the darkest

Chart 5.3 – Adjectives with two syllables

Adjectives	Comparative	Superlative
lucky	luckier than	the luckiest
happy	happier than	the happiest
lovely	lovelier than	the loveliest

Chart 5.4 – Adjectives with two or more syllables

Adjectives	Comparative	Superlative
tiring	more tiring than	the most tiring
exact	more exact than	the most exact
tragic	more tragic than	the most tragic
beautiful	more beautiful than	the most beautiful
expensive	more expensive than	the most expensive
comfortable	more comfortable than	the most comfortable

Chart 5.5 – Irregular, comparative and superlative forms

Simple	Comparative	Superlative
bad	worse than	the worst
good	better than	the best
well	better than	the best
far	farther, further than	the farthest
little	less than	the least
much	more than	the most
many	more than	the most

Exercises

7. Rewrite the sentences keeping the same meaning:
   a) Yesterday was hotter than today.
      Today _____
   b) Marketing is more interesting than Finance.
      Finance _____

c) Peter's salary is higher than Paul's salary.
   Paul's salary is _____
d) English is more useful than Dutch.
   Dutch _____
e) Peter earns less than Paul.
   Paul _____
f) His Spanish is better than his French.
   His French _____
g) Jane's office isn't as large as my office.
   My office is _____

8. Complete the blanks with the superlative of the adjective in bold:
   a) Silvia is an extremely **efficient** employee. She is _____ employee in her company.
   b) IBM was founded in 1889. No other computer manufacturer is as **old** as IBM. It is _____ computer manufacturer in the world.
   c) That shop is **bigger** than all the other shops. It is _____ shop in the street.
   d) O Boticário is a very **profitable** franchise in Brasil. In fact, many people think it is the _____ franchise in our country.
   e) Tina is a very **good** worker. In fact, she was elected _____ worker in our company.
   f) The B&D serves very bad **food**. In fact, it is _____ restaurant in town.

Curiosidades

Observe os seguintes adjetivos:

hot – ho**tt**er – the ho**tt**est
big – bi**gg**er – the bi**gg**est
lucky – luck**i**er – the luck**i**est
healthy – health**i**er – the health**i**est

Com base nesses exemplos, note que, no comparativo de superioridade e no superlativo de superioridade:

» Quando os adjetivos são monossílabos e terminam em uma consoante seguida por uma vogal e por outra consoante, dobra-se a consoante final, como nos exemplos do primeiro tipo:

hot – ho**tt**er – the ho**tt**est
big – bi**gg**er – the bi**gg**est

» Quando os adjetivos de duas sílabas terminam em *y*, precedido por uma consoante, troca-se o *y* pela vogal *i* e acrescenta-se o sufixo *er*, como nos exemplos do segundo tipo:

lucky – luck**i**er – the luck**i**est
healthy – health**i**er – the health**i**est

Exercise Approaching Collocations

9. Match the columns:
   a) big
   b) best
   c) good
   d) far
   e) wear
   f) well, badly
   g) high, low

   ( ) casual or smart clothes
   ( ) away
   ( ) luck
   ( ) seller
   ( ) heels
   ( ) deal
   ( ) dressed

Síntese do capítulo

No presente capítulo, abordamos dois assuntos distintos, porém essenciais para o ensino-aprendizagem da língua inglesa. Primeiramente, lidamos com verbos no futuro. Em seguida, observamos os adjetivos e como eles ficam nos graus comparativo e superlativo. Durante o desenvolvimento do capítulo, foram apresentados textos e vários exercícios para que os assuntos em pauta pudessem ser mais bem compreendidos e fixados.

Refeições na empresa

No dia a dia do profissional que trabalha em um ambiente empresarial, é comum que ele necessite fazer reservas em restaurantes ou providenciar refeições durante eventos, não só almoços e jantares, mas também os famosos *coffee breaks*, que acontecem nos intervalos de congressos, oficinas, palestras ou treinamentos.

A LITTLE BIT OF READING

Food and drink menu

Let's see an example of a typical american menu.

Breakfast Menu[1]
- Seasonal fresh fruit
- Bowl of cereal
- Pancakes
- Waffles

---

[1] Adaptado de Brasil Restaurant, 2012.

Continental Breakfast
- Assorted seasonal fruit
- Choice of croissant, muffin, danish or toast
- Coffee
- Choice of juice (orange, pineapple, apple, grapefruit)

American Breakfast
- 2 farm fresh eggs (any style: poached, fried, scrambled, cooked, omelette)
- Sausages
- Bacon
- Toast
- Coffee
- Choice of juice

Lunch Menu
- Soup du jour
- House Salad (lettuce, avocado, tomato, bacon, blue cheese, roasted garlic vinaigrette)
- Shrimp cocktail
- Chef's Caesar (with parmesan and homemade croutons, chicken, salmon, shrimp)
- Steak burger with caramelized onions
- Smoked turkey
- Omelette du Jour (served with a green salad)
- Roast chicken with asparagus or spinach
- Pasta with tomato sauce

Main Course

Steak (served with Garden Salad and appropriate starch and vegetable)

Salmon filet with mushroom risotto.

Chicken breast (with a fresh tomato and spinach cream sauce, mashed potatoes and fresh vegetables)

Filet mignon (grilled with mashed potatoes, roasted mushrooms and fresh vegetable)

Dinner Menu

Starters
- Soups (vegetable, onion)
- Chicken wings

Salads
- Fresh garden salad
- Spinach Salad
- Caesar Salad
- Greek Salad

As we can observe, the meals are not very different from the ones in Brazil – except that Americans have a bigger breakfast. But it is also offered a continental breakfast, which is simpler.

A LITTLE BIT OF GRAMMAR

Modal verbs

Denominamos *modal verbs* um grupo especial de verbos que usamos antes de outros verbos para expressar certos significados, indicando, por exemplo, permissão, habilidade, possibilidade e certeza.

Os *modal verbs* possuem uma forma gramatical diferente daquela comumente apresentada por outros verbos. Por exemplo, não se acrescenta a letra *s* à terceira pessoa do singular – dizemos *he can* e não *he cans*. Outro ponto interessante é que eles também não podem ser usados em todos os tempos verbais; geralmente, apresentam somente uma ou duas formas, presente e passado. Logo, constituem um grupo especial de verbos auxiliares.

| Can   Could   May   Might   Shall   Should   Will   Would   Must |

Vamos agora descrever as particularidades do uso de verbos desse grupo:

- » Infinitivos sem a partícula *to*: após os *modals verbs*, usa-se o verbo no infinitivo sem a partícula *to*.
    - › He **can** speak Italian.
    - › He **can't** speak Italian.
    - › **Can** he speak Italian?

- » Não se acrescenta *s* à terceira pessoa do singular.
    - › John **may** be late.
    - › John **may not** come in.
    - › **May** he come in?

- » Não se usa *do*, *does*, *do not* ou *does not* em frases interrogativas e negativas.
    - › **Should** you call him tonight?
    - › You **should not** arrive late.

- » Não apresentam infinitivo, gerúndio ou particípio, ou seja, ***to can***, ***maying***, ***musted*** são formas **erradas**.

Uso dos *modal verbs*

O significado dos *modal verbs* depende do contexto.

- » *Can* pode assumir vários significados. São eles:
    - › **Habilidade** (no sentido de saber executar a ação)
        - › You **can deal** with the computer.
        - › He **can't deal** with the computer.
        - › **Can** they **deal** with the computer?
    - › **Permissão**
        - › **Can** I **leave** early?
        - › You **can't leave** now.
        - › He **can go** now.

- › **Oferta**
  - › **Can** I **help you** with the report? (Posso te ajudar...?)
  - › He **can help you** with this.

» Usamos *may* e *might* quando achamos que algo é possível ou quando não temos certeza sobre algo.
  - › He **may win** the next election. (é possível)
  - › I **may/might have** some news for you next week. (talvez eu tenha)

» Entretanto, quando usamos no negativo, *may not* e *might not*, esses verbos descrevem algo incerto, não impossibilidades.
  - › We **may/might not have** time to finish the paper on time. (não sabemos)

» Usamos *could* quando não temos certeza, especialmente com o verbo *to be*.
  - › He **could be late** because of the traffic. (talvez)

» Podemos usar o modal *can't* quando temos certeza que algo é impossível.
  - › Paul **can't come** to the meeting, because he's in Europe. (é impossível)

» *Can't* e *must* podem ser usados também quando deduzimos algum fato ou temos certeza de algo.
  - › He's late. He **must be** stuck in traffic. (tenho quase certeza, pois nunca chega atrasado)
  - › She **can't be** in Europe. I saw her today at work. (tenho certeza de que ela não viajou)

» Quando precisamos explicar que alguma coisa é extremamente necessária, usamos *must* ou *have to*. Apesar de *have to* não ser considerado um *modal verb*, também o usamos nesse caso.
  - › You **have to finish** the work before going home.

» *Must* não é usado com tanta frequência no inglês americano. Geralmente, demonstra um sentido de urgência e obrigação mais forte do que *have to*, especialmente quando a palavra *must* é enfatizada na fala.
  - › Secretaries **must be** punctual and organized.
  - › We **must stop** using his office! (precisamos parar)

» *Mustn't* (*must not*) e *don't have to* têm significados diferentes. *Mustn't* descreve uma ação que é proibida. É usado em documentos oficiais e em avisos, bem como em advertências e alertas.
  - › You *mustn't play* with matches. (Você não deve brincar com fósforos).

› You **mustn't step** on the grass. (É proibido pisar na grama).

» **Don't have to** descreve uma ação que não é necessária.
› You **don't have to** finish the work today. It's not due till next week.

» **Should** e **shouldn't** expressam a ideia do emissor sobre o que é uma boa ou uma má ação. Pode ser uma opinião, mas geralmente é usado para dar conselhos.
› (I think) You **should do** your job more carefully. (conselho)
› (I think) The police **should arrest** vandals. (opinião)

» Também podemos expressar que esperamos algo acontecer.
› They **should arrive** on the 6 o'clock flight. (expectativa)

» Shouldn't pode também ser usado para mostrar obrigação.
› You **shouldn't drive** faster than the speed limit.

> Esse uso de *shouldn't* não é tão forte quanto *mustn't* e, às vezes, o seu uso é mais apropriado.

Exercise

1. Choose the correct word or phrase in each sentence:

   Example:
   Look at those clouds. I think it can / (might) / must rain.

   a) This is not possible! The answer can't / mustn't / may not be this.
   b) Excellent job! The boss may / must / might be pleased!
   c) I have no idea where Susan is. She could / must be anywhere!

d) I suppose it's possible. He might / has to / must get the job.
e) I'm not sure. I must not / may not be able to get to work on time.
f) That can't / mustn't / may not be true. It didn't happen yesterday.
g) Liz isn't here yet. She can / must be on her way.
h) There's someone at the door. It might / mustn't be the mailman.
i) Sorry, she can't / may go out. She has to finish her work.

Preposições

Preposições indicam a relação entre substantivos, pronomes e outras palavras em uma sentença. Geralmente, aparecem antes de um substantivo e nunca apresentam variações referentes ao gênero e número da palavra com a qual se relacionam.

Vamos examinar algumas classes de preposições.

Prepositions of time

Usamos as preposições de tempo para indicar quando algo acontece, aconteceu ou acontecerá.

» **At**
   › Horas
      › **At** 6 o'clock.
   › Feriados
      › **At** Christmas; **at** Easter; **at** the weekend.
   › Expressões de tempo
      › **At** the moment; **at** present; **at** dawn; **at** noon; **at** night; **at** midnight.
» **In**
   › Meses
      › **In** April; **in** June.
   › Estações do ano
      › **In** spring; **in** winter; **in** summer; **in** autumn.
   › Anos
      › **In** 1994; **in** 2009.
   › Séculos.
      › **In** the 21st century.
   › Nas expressões
      › **in** the morning; **in** the afternoon; **in** the evening, **in** an hour; **in** a minute; **in** a week; **in** a few days; **in** a month; in a year etc.
» **On**
   › Dias da semana
      › **On** Monday; **on** Friday; **on** New Year's Day.
   › Datas completas
      › **On** July 4th.

> Parte específica do dia
>> **On** Monday morning; **on** Sunday evening.
> Adjetivo + dia
>> **On** a cold day; **on** a nice day.

Prepositions of place

Usamos as preposições de lugar para expressar onde alguém ou alguma coisa está.

» **On**
> The customer is sitting **on** the sofa.

» **Under**
> The cat is hiding **under** the table.

» **In front of**
> The chair is **in front of** the window.

» **Behind**
> The garbage is **behind** the door.

» **Beside** ou **next to**
  › The assistant is standing **beside** / **next to** the manager.

» **Near**
  › The car is **near** the truck.

» **At**
  › He is sitting **at** his desk.

» **In**
  › The pencils are **in** the drawer.

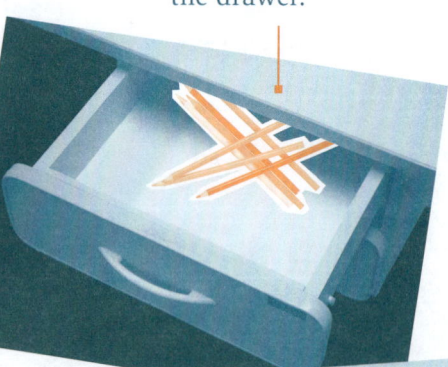

» **Between**
  › The stapler is **between** the pencil case and the agenda.

» **Among**
  › The report is **among** the files.

» **Opposite**
  › The sofa is **opposite** the chair.

As preposições *at*, *in* e *on* também são usadas da seguinte maneira:
» **At**
  › Nas expressões
    › **at** school; **at** the university; **at** college; **at** work; **at** home; **at** the airport; **at** the top of…; **at** the bottom of…; **at** the moment.
  › Em endereços completos
    › He works **at** 15 Main Street.
» **In**
  › Nas expressões
    › **in** the middle; **in** the air; **in** the sky; **in** bed; **in** (the) hospital; **in** prison; **in** a newspaper/ magazine/ book; **in** a picture; **in** a street; **in** the world.
  › Em nomes de cidades, países e continentes
    › **in** Paris; **in** Brazil; **in** South América.
» **On**
  › Nas expressões
    › **on** the left/right; **on** the first/second floor; **on** a chair.
  › Em endereços, quando mencionamos somente a rua/avenida
    › **on** Main Street; **on** Second Avenue.

Prepositions of movement

Usamos as preposições de movimento para indicar a direção em que alguém ou alguma coisa está se movimentando.

- » **Along**
  › The truck is going **along** the expressway.
- » **Across** 
  › They are walking **across** the street.
- » **Up** 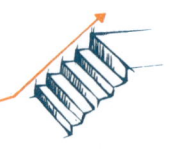
  › The students are going **up** the stairs.
- » **Down** 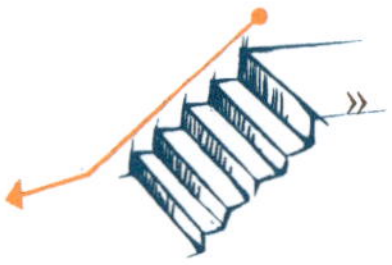
  › The men are coming **down** the steps.
- » **Into** 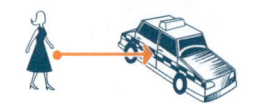
  › The woman is getting **into** the taxi.
- » **Out of** 
  › The lawyer is coming **out of** the Court building.
- » **Over** 
  › The train is going **over** the bridge.
- » **From … to …** 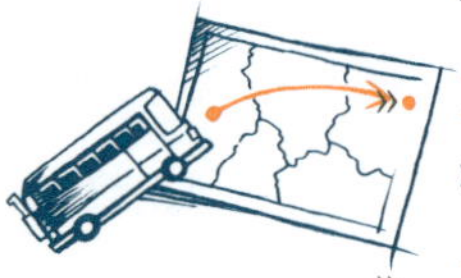
  › The bus is going **from** New York **to** Boston.
- » **Round** 
  › The carrousel is going **round and round**.
- » **Onto** 
  › She's climbing **onto** the boat.
- » **Through** 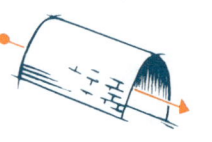
  › The car is going **through** the tunnel.

Há dois *modal verbs* que não foram mencionados, pois são raramente usados nos Estados Unidos: *shall* e *ought to*. Tanto *shall* como *ought to* são extremamente formais e estão em desuso no inglês americano. No inglês britânico, porém, ambas as formas são utilizadas.

- » We **shall** leave quite early tomorrow. (britânico)
- » We **should/must** leave quite early tomorrow. (americano)

- » **Shall** we start the meeting? (britânico)
- » **Let's** start the meeting? (americano)

- » We **ought to** finish the paper by tomorrow morning. (formal, britânico)
- » We **should** finish the paper by tomorrow morning. (americano)

Outro ponto que gostaríamos de mencionar é que a partícula *to* não é usada após os seguintes *modal verbs*: *would, may, might, shall* e *must*.

» I **would** like to leave early.
» He **may** come in today.
» It **might** rain.
» Who **shall** we invite for the meeting?
» Secretaries **must** be patient!

Já o *modal verb ought* é sempre seguido da partícula *to*:
» You **ought to** stay.

O significado da sentença anterior é semelhante ao da seguinte:
» You **should** stay.

Exercise

2. Agora que já observamos os vários usos das preposições, complete algumas frases com a preposição correta:
   a) Diana is painting her office _____ the moment.
      ( ) at
      ( ) in
   b) The boss is sitting _____ the sofa.
      ( ) on
      ( ) into
   c) They're checking the map to see if there is another way of getting to town instead of going _____ the forest.
      ( ) out
      ( ) through
   d) Planes always fly _____ our office.
      ( ) over
      ( ) under
   e) We're taking the bus _____ Rome _____ Naples.
      ( ) to... from...
      ( ) from... to...
   f) The post office is just _____ the corner.
      ( ) around
      ( ) through
   g) He went _____ the stairs from the 17th floor.
      ( ) on
      ( ) down
   h) He is tired because he has just ran _____ the stairs.
      ( ) up
      ( ) into
   i) The new office is _____ the old building.
      ( ) near
      ( ) out of

j) They work _____ 25 Old Town Road.
   ( ) on
   ( ) at

A LITTLE BIT OF READING

Etiquette tips for the business dinner

Why **should** we learn dinner table etiquette? Many of today's business meetings, sales meetings, and job interviews take place over the dinner table. Sometimes these meetings are at a restaurant, and other times they are in a corporate dining hall, so it is always useful to know which fork to eat your salad with.

Top ten dinner etiquette rules

1) **Start on the outside** – On a properly set table you usually see a series of forks on the left side of your plate and spoons and knives on your right. The very simple rule is: the cutlery farthest away from your plate is for the first course.

2) **Build bridges** – When you put your knives, forks, and spoons down, place the entire utensil on the plate (bridge). When you are finished, place your knife and fork together in the center of the plate, which will let your server know you have finished.

3) **Cutting your food** – You **should** always use both your knife and fork together.

4) **Eating soup** – You **should** bring the spoon to your mouth and drink the soup from the edge of the spoon and do not put the whole spoon in to your mouth. And, of course, do not slurp.

5) **Napkins** – They **should** be unfolded and placed on your lap. It is never acceptable to tuck your napkin in to the front of your shirt.

6) **Glasses** – Normally you will have two or more glasses at the table. Your glasses are on the right upper side of your plate. You can have up to four glasses. The top left glass with a larger bowl is for red wine. Directly below that you will find the white wine glass, which will be smaller. At the top right, you will find a champagne glass and the water glass is on the bottom right.

7) **Sitting** – You **should not** sit before your host or hostess. If there is no host, then you should wait for the oldest person at the table to sit first before you.

8) **Starting to eat** – You **should not** pick up your fork and begin eating until the host, hostess, or older person at the table begins. It is advisable not to start eating until everyone has been served even if your food is getting cold.

9) Spitting food out – If you take a mouthful of food which contains something you cannot swallow, you **should** remove the piece of food by whichever means it entered your mouth.

10) Bread and butter – When you begin to eat bread or any other food from a common bowl, you **should** offer the bread basket to the person on your left and then begin passing the bowl around the table to the right. If you are having bread with your meal there will usually be a small side plate on the left hand side of your place setting. Bread **should** be torn with your fingers and never be cut with a knife if offered in the loaf form. Tear a bite sized piece off with your fingers. Use your butter knife to transfer a sufficient portion of butter for your bread, making sure that you get enough. Place it on the side of your side plate, and butter each piece of bread as you eat it.

Source: Adapted from Coleman, 2012.

Exercises

3. No texto intitulado "Negotiating", no Capítulo 5, há vários *modal verbs* destacados. Relacione o modal verb extraído desse texto à sua função:
   a) may (be); may (last)   ( ) strong possibility (pode)
   b) should (get prepared)   ( ) necessity (precisa)
   c) might or might not   ( ) some possibility (pode)
      (get some extra money)
   d) should (simulate)   ( ) advice (deve)
   e) need (to meet)
   f) should (be prepared)

4. Já no texto sobre etiqueta à mesa, intitulado "The top ten etiquette tips for the business dinner or interview", há apenas um *modal verb* (*should*). De acordo com a explicação sobre o uso desse tipo de verbo, qual é a função que este assume no texto?
   a) Possibilidade.
   b) Habilidade.
   c) Sugestão e/ou conselho.
   d) Obrigação.
   e) Proibição.

5. Read the sentences and mark them correct (C) or incorrect (I) and rewrite the incorrect ones:
   a) ( ) She cans drive a car.
   _____
   b) ( ) Can you to type?
   _____
   c) ( ) You don't must open that door.
   _____

6 • Refeições na empresa

d) ( ) Must you go?
_____

e) ( ) Last year I must work on Saturdays.
_____

f) ( ) When do you have to leave?
_____

g) ( ) We mustn't pay now, but we can if we want to.
_____

h) ( ) Would you like coming out with us?
_____

i) ( ) I should tell you everything.
_____

6. Complete with the correct preposition:
   a) I'll see you _____ Tuesday.
   b) Are you going away _____ Christmas?
   c) I'll wait for you _____ the cinema.
   d) I walked _____ the street and went _____ the station.
   e) A bird flew _____ the window of my office.
   f) Mary went _____ the stairs to the 10th floor.
   g) What time are we arriving _____ London?
   h) The meeting starts _____ 9:45 a.m.
   i) The company is _____ the park. You can walk there.
   j) The letter *C* comes _____ the letters *B* and *D*.

Exercises Approaching Collocations

7. Complete the sentences with a word from the box:

   | jam | course | job | stuck | menu | limit |
   | on the grass | breakfast | lunch | the computer |

   a) There is a notice outside the company saying: You mustn't step _____.

   b) I like to do my _____ early in the morning, before the other employees arrive at the company.

   c) She is a good assistant, but she can't deal with _____ very well.

   d) On Friday evening, there is always a terrible traffic _____ in the motorway.

   e) I was late for work because we ran out of light and I got _____ in the lift.

f) When I go to a restaurant I usually have meat as the main _____.
g) Where do you usually have _____ at noon? At home or at work?
h) What is the speed _____ in Germany?
i) When I travel abroad, I prefer to have the continental _____.
j) My boss likes to have a look at the vegetarian _____, as he doesn't eat meat.

Síntese do capítulo

Neste capítulo, abordamos dois assuntos diferentes de grande importância no aprendizado da língua inglesa. Primeiramente, discutimos o uso dos *modal verbs* e as peculiaridades destes. Em segundo lugar, trabalhamos o uso de preposições, as quais os estudantes também costumam apresentar certas dificuldades em empregar corretamente e nem sempre são compreendidas de maneira lógica – especialmente em razão de algumas assumirem mais de um significado. Apresentamos explicações e exercícios para fixar a aprendizagem, bem como textos referentes às refeições no ambiente empresarial, com diferentes cardápios e regras relativas a como se comportar em um almoço ou jantar.

O escritório/The office

Como o escritório é o local onde os profissionais de negócios passam a maior parte de seus horários de trabalho, nós o consideramos um lugar de extrema relevância. Por isso, dedicamos este capítulo a descrevê-lo.

Certamente, há vários escritórios diferentes, uma vez que dependem, principalmente, do tipo de negócio que representam. Vejamos o *chat* a seguir, em que dois tipos de escritórios são descritos pelos respectivos gerentes de vendas.

A LITTLE BIT OF READING

Moving offices

John: Hi, Joe. Have you moved and fixed your office yet?

Joe: Hi, John. I haven't finished it yet, but I have just filled all the customers' folders in the new cabinet. It's great! It's much better than the old one.

John: But you still have loads of things to organize, don't you?

Joe: Sure!!! You can't imagine the mess. But I have always been patient, so I don't mind. In fact, I have just connected the printer and it's working ok! I can already access all my customers' accounts. What a relief!

John: Where have you put the printer?

Joe: Oh, there is plenty of room for everything here. Actually, my table is large enough for the computer and the printer. And there is a very good point: it's quite airy here and well-lit too. What about yours? Have you already moved to a more modern office?

John: I haven't moved yet, but I am going to start organizing everything so that I can move next week. Do you have your own office or do you have to share it with the sales staff?

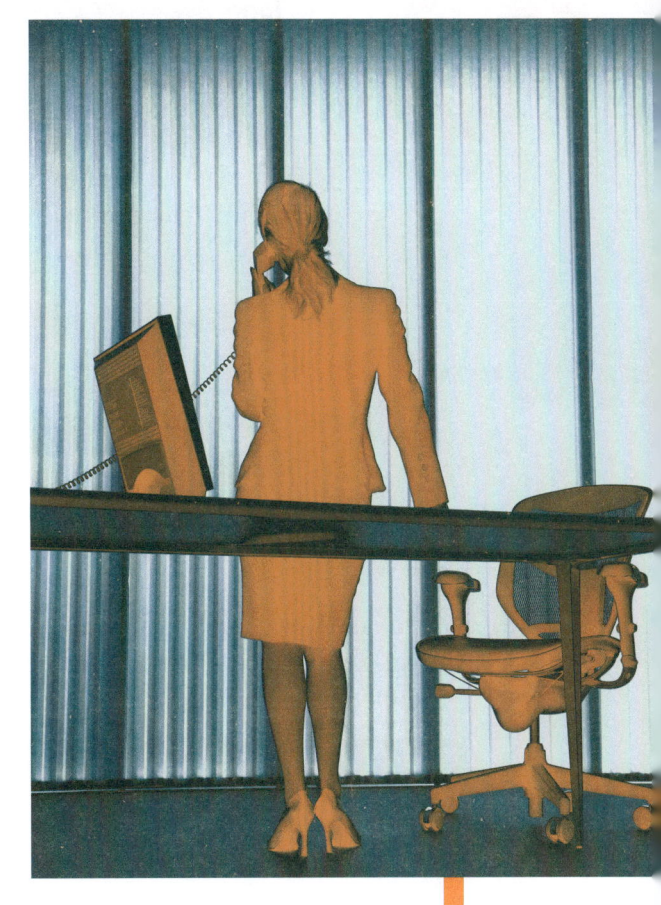

Joe: Thank goodness it's my own office, so I have a lot of privacy. What about you?

John: I am going to share the room with three senior sales people, but I am quite satisfied because I hate being alone.

Joe: Anyway, let's have a cup of coffee as soon as we have some free time, ok?

John: Of course! Come and give me some ideas on where to put my personal belongings, ok?

Joe: Don't worry! I will! Bye!

John: Bye!

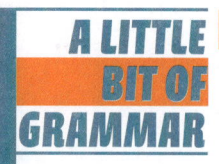

A LITTLE BIT OF GRAMMAR

Present Perfect

O *Present Perfect* é o tempo verbal que tem como característica fazer a união entre ações que aconteceram no passado e ações que acontecem no presente. Em outras palavras, como o nome *Present Perfect* já diz, trata-se de um tempo verbal relacionado ao presente.

Vejamos como o *Present Perfect* é formado:

> Present Perfect = auxiliary *have* + *main verb* in the Past Participle

Uma vez que o verbo *have/has* é usado como auxiliar, a forma interrogativa é formada com a inversão entre o sujeito e o verbo auxiliar, e a forma negativa, com o acréscimo da partícula de negação *not* após *have/has*.

Exercise

1. No *chat* anterior, John e Joe usam o *Present Perfect* três vezes na forma afirmativa, três na interrogativa e duas na negativa. Localize tais usos e complete o quadro com alguns exemplos a seguir:

Present Perfect affirmative	Present Perfect interrogative	Present Perfect negative
		X

No que tange ao uso do *Present Perfect*, deve-se observar as regras mencionadas a seguir[1]:

---

[1] Visando à ampliação do seu vocabulário, as regras de uso do *Present Perfect* serão apresentadas em inglês.

We use the Present Perfect tense when we are concerned with the present effects of something which happened at an indefinite time in the past:

- I'm afraid **I've forgotten** my book.
- **Have** you **heard** from the accountant recently?

Sometimes, the present effects are important because the events are very recent:

- Karen **has just passed** the Bar exams.
- Beth **has just had** a promotion.

We also use the Present Perfect when we are thinking of a time which started in the past and is still continuing:

- **Have** you really **worked** here **for** ten years?
- He **has worked** here **since** 1987.

We also use the Present Perfect in time clauses, when we are talking about something which will be done at some time in the future:

- Tell me when you **have finished**.
- I'll write to you as soon as **I have heard** from the treasurer.

Vale enfatizar que o Present Perfect pode corresponder a mais de um tempo verbal em português. Por isso, é preciso que atentemos para essas regras de uso. Para que você possa compreender melhor, vamos efetuar uma análise contrastiva entre o português e o inglês, usando o *Present Perfect* e o tempo correspondente em português:

- **Moro** em Curitiba há quatro anos e **trabalho** na Facinter desde 2007. (Presente do Indicativo)
- I **have lived** in Curitiba for four years, and I **have worked** at Facinter since 2007. (Present Perfect)

- Desculpe, mas **esqueci** minhas chaves e agora não posso abrir a sala de conferências. (Pretérito Perfeito do Indicativo)
- Sorry, but I **have forgotten** my keys and now I can't open the conference room. (Present Perfect)

- Você **já almoçou**? (Pretérito Perfeito do Indicativo)
- **Have** you **already had lunch**? (Present Perfect)

- Mary **acabou de fazer** um café. Sirva-se! (Pretérito Perfeito do Indicativo)
- Mary **has just made** some coffee. Help yourself! (Present Perfect)

- Informe-me quando você **tiver terminado** o relatório. (Futuro Composto do Subjuntivo)
- Tell me when you **have finished** the report. (Presente Perfect)

Usando *for* e *since*

For

We use this preposition to refer to an amount of time – *years, months, hours, minutes* etc. (quantidade de tempo – anos, meses, horas, minutos etc.).

The preposition *for* can be used in sentences with several verb tenses, but we use it mainly when we talk about:

1. Finished actions in the past, so the verb is also in the past.
   › Mary worked here from 2000 to 2002. She doesn't work here anymore.
   › Mary worked here **for** three years.

2. Actions that started in the past but continue until the present, so the verb is usually in the *Present Perfect*.
   › Mary started working here three years ago and she still works here.
   › She has worked here **for** three years.

Since

We use this preposition when we refer to the beginning of a period of time, that is, when we talk about something that started in the past and continues until the present. Consequently, the verb is usually in the Present Perfect.
› Mary started working here in 2006 and she still works here.
› She has worked here **since** 2006.

Exercises

2. Rewrite the following sentences using the indicated words:
   a) It is now 11 o'clock. George has worked in the lab for two hours. (since)

   b) George and Anne have been partners since 1946. (for)

   c) I have learned English for three years. (since)

   d) I have worked in this company since 1980. (for)

   e) George has been the company's CEO for ten years. (since)

3. **Complete the sentences with *since* or *for*:**
   a) It has rained _____ I got up this morning.
   b) Tom has been a policeman _____ 20 years.
   c) Have you travelled _____ a long time?
   d) Ann has been on holiday _____ three days.
   e) That's a very old computer. I've had it _____ ages.

A LITTLE BIT OF READING

Tips on answering the phone at work

Being able to answer the phone in a polite way is an essential part of communication with others. However, it may be a hard task, mainly if the speaker is nervous and not very secure about what to say, so here are a few tips on answering the telephone at work politely.

» Speak clearly.
» Use the company's preferred greeting, if there is one. If not, state the name of the business.
» Be polite and responsive, giving the caller your full attention. Remember that, at that moment, you're the company's representative.
» Be as helpful as possible, even if it's not exactly your job to answer the phone.
» Learn how to use the phone's features smoothly.
» Ask permission first, if you must put the caller on hold: "Would you mind holding for a minute?".
» Don't forget the caller is waiting. Ask them periodically if they'd like to continue to hold, call back or leave a message.
» Transfer the caller to someone who can help, if you can't.
» Take a good message, if applicable, and pass it on to the recipient.
» Thank the caller.

Source: Adaptado de Phone Sense, 2012.

Leia o diálogo a seguir e preste atenção às expressões destacadas, que poderiam ser repetidas em uma situação semelhante:

> **Kate**: Good morning (afternoon/evening), Manchester Enterprises, Kate Jones speaking.
> **Lyz**: Hello, **this is** Lyz Smith from AVG International. Could you put me through to John Martin, please?
> **Kate**: I'm afraid he's on another line at the moment. Could you hold on the line or should I take a message?
> **Lyz**: **I've tried to get through** several times but **it's always engaged**, so I will hold on.
> **Kate**: Mr. Martin **has just hung up**. I will **put you through** now.
> **Lyz**: Thank you.

Source: Adaptado de Phone Sense, 2012.

Como podemos observar, após o cumprimento, ambas se identificaram e deixaram claro qual empresa estariam representando no momento. Como a pessoa solicitada estava em outra ligação, a atendente ofereceu as opções "aguardar na linha" e "deixar um recado". No final, a ligação foi passada para a pessoa solicitada.

Exercises

4. Para fixar o vocabulário referente à conversa telefônica, relacione as colunas:
    a) Kate Jones speaking ( ) a linha está ocupada
    b) Take a message ( ) passar a ligação
    c) Hold on ( ) Kate Jones na linha
    d) Put someone through ( ) anotar um recado
    e) The line is engaged (busy) ( ) aguardar na linha
    f) Hang up ( ) desligar o telefone

5. The Present Perfect is frequently confused with the Simple Past. To make it clear when each one should be used, let's relate the following sentences:
    a) Have you seen the job offers in the paper?
    b) Did you see the job offers in the paper?
    c) My former boss has lived in the USA for 10 years.
    d) My former boss lived in the USA for 10 years.
    e) Did you have a coffee break?
    f) Have you had a coffee break?
    g) The computer technician didn't come.
    h) The computer technician hasn't come.

    ( ) It is 8:00 a.m.
    ( ) It is 8:00 p.m.
    ( ) The staff are still waiting for the business trainer.
    ( ) The staff waited for the business trainer for some time and the training class is now over.

( ) There are good job offers in the paper this week.
( ) There were good job offers in the paper last week.
( ) She worked in the USA from 1995 to 2005.
( ) She still works in the USA.

6. **Use the words given and make sentences in the Present Perfect:**
   a) Bill / to work / in New York / 1990. (since)

   b) I / to work / as an engineer. (for a long time)

   c) They / to attend / the training program. (already)

   d) I / to meet / Mr. Watson. (never) (before)

   e) She / to post / the Christmas cards to the customers. (yet)

   f) That is / the longest / letter / I / to write to a company. (ever)

   g) You / to be / Madrid on business? (ever)

   h) Tom / to want / to be / a famous / lawyer. (always)

   i) The sales staff / to eat / in that restaurant. (many times)

   j) Mr. Smith / to be / to the USA on business (for three times)

Curiosidades

Notamos que o *Present Perfect* é muitas vezes usado quando determinados vocábulos, como os destacados nos exemplos a seguir, também estão presentes:

» Have you **ever** visited the new branch?

» My brother has **already** given a presentation at work, but my sister has **never** done it.

» Have the special guests arrived **yet**?

» We have been studying Computer Science **since** last year.

» We have been studying Computer Science **for** one year.

» My boss has read the Steve Jobs biography **many times**.

» I haven't been to the European company **yet**.

» Listen! The phone has **just** rung.

Quando nos referimos a uma ação que continua desde algum tempo no passado até o presente, muitas vezes podemos usar o *Present Perfect* ou o *Present Perfect Continuous*, que é formado pelo verbo auxiliar *have/has* seguido pelo particípio passado do verbo *to be* (*been*) e do gerúndio do verbo principal. Por exemplo:

» I **have taught** Finance for many years.

ou

» I **have been teaching** Finance for many years.

Uma vez que o material de escritório é vasto e diverso, sugerimos os seguintes *sites*:

ELFNET. **Office Supplies Picture Vocabulary**. Disponível em: <http://www.eflnet.com/vocab/officesupplies_vocabulary.php>. Acesso em: 10 mar. 2012.

ENGLISH AT HOME. **Office Vocabulary**. Disponível em: <http://www.english-at-home.com/vocabulary/office-vocabulary>. Acesso em: 10 mar. 2012.

THE ENGLISH WEB. Disponível em: <http://www.theenglishweb.com/articles/office-vocabulary.php>. Acesso em: 10 mar. 2012.

Exercise Approaching Collocations

7. Complete the text with the expressions in the box:

| customers' accounts | get through | hang up | sales staff | taking messages |
| hard tasks | what a relief | hold the line | customer's folders | don't worry |

The new office has been opened. The entire staff were able to (a) _____ the first week, working very hard. The (b) _____ had some (c) _____ to take care of, like (d) _____, and asking customers to please (e) _____ and wait a little and not to (f) _____. They were filing away (g) _____ all week long. The (h) _____ were all called up by their respective sales reps.

So, they told everyone: (i) _____, we're doing business as usual. At the end of the first week they had all in order and said: (j) _____!

Síntese do capítulo

Neste capítulo, abordamos um assunto considerado complexo por alguns alunos: o *Present Perfect*. Entretanto, após as explicações referentes a esse tempo verbal e os exercícios sugeridos, esperamos que você tenha aprendido a usá-lo corretamente. Em relação à parte lexical, apresentamos a linguagem comumente utilizada em uma conversa telefônica e no dia a dia de um escritório.

8
Viagens de negócios

Uma tarefa importante no mundo corporativo é organizar viagens de negócios. Isso envolve várias etapas, desde uma simples reunião de negócios na mesma cidade até a reserva de hotéis, carros e passagens aéreas, tanto nacionais como internacionais.

Nesse sentido, vamos apresentar um texto sobre o preparo de uma viagem de negócios.

A LITTLE BIT OF READING

Business Trip

The business trip can be a simple car ride to another company in the same city, or an extensive trip to other countries for an extended time period. It is necessary to be ready for either one, preparing all the arrangements that precede it.

Below, we will present a list of tasks that should be done, so that the business trip goes on smoothly and without any complications.

How to Prepare It

» Write down in a diary all your appointments, the names of the people you will meet and their respective positions, addresses, telephones, hotels etc.
» Make sure that all the airline reservations are confirmed, as well as hotels and transportation, if necessary.
» Make sure that the documents are in order with any visas to foreign countries, when required.

- » The schedule should have some free time in case you meet someone and would like to have an appointment with this person, or to know the place and its culture, which can be interesting.
- » It's important, also: to check on the country's market, to get to know its tendencies, to visit fairs which are of interest for the company, and to visit other companies.
- » Buy some *souvenirs* to give as presents to the people you are meeting. It is part of the business etiquette.
- » Make sure you take the proper clothes for the various appointments and check for the usual weather and temperature for the necessary clothing.
- » Check for the country's exchange rate, and the business etiquette you should be aware of, like: how to shake hands etc.
- » Check on the budget available for the trip and if it is necessary to request a cash advance.
- » If you are going to make a presentation, remember to organize the slides.
- » Prepare ten important phrases in the language of the country being visited and write them out, so you can take along.

Source: Adaptado de Roseland, 2012.

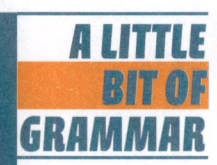

A LITTLE BIT OF GRAMMAR

Used to e o uso do infinitivo e do gerúndio

A expressão *used to* pode ser empregada tanto para referir-se a situações que aconteceram no passado com regularidade como para indicar algo que estamos acostumados a fazer. Veja como utilizar essa expressão:

- » *Used to + infinitive* – É empregado para falar de situações que aconteceram várias vezes no passado, ou seja, hábitos no passado que não existem ou não acontecem mais no presente.
  - › He **used to study** economics, but he stopped.
  - › Pat didn't **use to work** in Chicago, she worked in Houston.
  - › Did the Beatles **use to have** long hair?

- » *Be/get used to + verb + ing* – É empregado para falar sobre hábitos e costumes.
  - › He **is used to playing** soccer in the USA.

  Implicitamente estamos dizendo:
  - › It is not a problem for him as he has done it many times.

Na sequência, você pode observar mais alguns exemplos. Todos dão a ideia de hábitos ou costumes rotineiros e não ações no passado:
- › They are used to jogging in the cold weather.
- › Are you used to working till late at night?
- › They got used to studying together.
- › We didn't get used to eating spinach.
- › Have they got used to working overtime?

Exercises

1. Put the verb into the correct form (*ing* or *infinitive*).

    Example:
    I am used to **doing** / I used to **do.**

    a) When he was a student, he used to _____ (walk) to the university every day.
    b) It took her a long time to get used to _____ (learn) to operate the fax machine.
    c) There used to _____ (be) a stationary store on this corner, but it was torn down.
    d) She's the boss. She's not used to _____ (be) told what to do.
    e) You'll have to get used to _____ (work) more if you want to get a promotion.
    f) We used to _____ (meet) the new students, when we were studying finances.
    g) Ron got hired very quickly. He is used to _____ (follow) rules.
    h) Tom used to _____ (go) to a lot of parties when he was a student.
    i) They got used to _____ (drive) on the left when living in England.
    j) After he was hired in the new company, he got used to _____ (stay) till late every day.

2. Após fazer e corrigir o exercício acima, releia as sentenças e escreva a letra *P* se a situação referir-se a uma ação que não acontece mais e a letra *H* se a ação relacionar-se à hábitos frequentes:

    a) ( )
    b) ( )
    c) ( )
    d) ( )
    e) ( )
    f) ( )
    g) ( )
    h) ( )
    i) ( )
    j) ( )

Uso de *too, enough, so* e *such*

As palavras *too, enough, so* e *such* são chamadas de *function words* e, geralmente, intensificam um adjetivo. Observe os exemplos a seguir:

- **Enough**
  - Before singular (uncountable) and plural nouns
    - Do you have **enough** money for the bus?
    - There aren't **enough** glasses for everyone.
  - After adjectives and adverbs
    - The room is big **enough** for two beds.
    - They are not walking fast **enough**.
  - It can also be used alone
    - I can lend you some money if you don't have **enough**.
- **Too**
  - Before adjectives to intensify them

    > too + adjective + verb in the infinitive

    - He's **too** tired to sing.
    - She **was** too afraid to speak.
- **So**
  - With an adjective without a noun
    - He was **so** tired after work.
    - The movie was **so** sad.
  - It can also be used before an adverb
    - He was **so** friendly.
    - They speak **so** quickly.
- **Such**
  - With an adjective and a noun
    - It was **such** a bad movie.
    - They had **such** a good time.

Exercises

3. Complete with *so* or *such*:
   a) Come on! Don't walk _____ fast.
   b) I've never read _____ an interesting book.
   c) It was _____ a boring movie that I fell asleep.
   d) The wind was _____ strong, it was difficult to walk.
   e) She has _____ beautiful eyes.

4. Now, complete with *too* or *enough*:
   a) Tom wants to buy a car, but he doesn't have _____ money.
   b) It's only a small car. There isn't _____ room for everybody.
   c) I can't drink this tea. It's _____ hot.
   d) Do you think I've got _____ qualifications for the job?
   e) Nobody could move the piano. It was _____ heavy.

A LITTLE BIT OF READING

Organizing business trips

When a business trip has to be organized, the following points should be found out first:

- » What is the purpose of the trip?
- » What is the destination? If many places have to be visited, then it is wise to plan this in a logical order, in order to save time and money.
- » Who is/are the person/people who has/have to travel and who are the people who will be visited?
- » If part of the trip is organized by others, good contact with the people who will do it is important, as you need to know what will be organized by whom.

- » Check if you have a margin on dates and times, as you might be able to save money on booking flights and hotels.
- » What is the budget, and, in some cases, what is the travel policy of the company?
- » The next step is about getting to know the following information.
- » Check the validity of the passport and scan it, and send it to a web mail address, so the information is always accessible.
- » If you have special dietary requirements, make sure to request when making reservations on the airline and hotels.
- » Will you need a driver's license, and possibly an international driving permit?
- » Do you smoke?
- » Do you need to take any medicines? If these are prescribed, then it is wise to have a letter from the doctor confirming the need

> for these medicines, in order to prevent problems while passing customs.
> » Depending on the destination, you need to find out if any special vaccines are necessary, for example TB vaccination, malaria vaccination, herpes vaccination or DTP vaccination.
> » Check whether it would be a good idea to have insurance. If necessary, take the right action.

Source: Adaptado de Professional Secretarial Services, 2012.

Other important information

Make sure that you have the following information for ready access: meetings, conferences, places to visit, local etiquette, local language, contact information of the people, companies and hotels involved.

> Other things which might be important to check:
> » Local time at destination.
> » Credit cards (Can your credit cards be used in the country of destination?).
> » The amount of luggage which can be taken.
> » Goods to declare at the customs, and items which cannot cross the border.
> » Other handy accessories for traveling.
> » What to wear when traveling.

Exercises

5. Complete each sentence with *used to* plus the verb in parentheses in the infinitive or gerund:
   a) The personnel department doesn't work overtime so much now, but it _____ (work) late every night.
   b) She _____ (give) lectures, but she doesn't anymore.
   c) We work in Los Angeles now, but we _____ (work) in San Francisco.
   d) Tom became the production director. He _____ (be) the manager.
   e) They're _____ (surf) the Internet every evening after work.
   f) He isn't _____ (stay) late at the office on weekends.
   g) You're _____ (talk) to people in Europe every morning.
   h) Sally got _____ (watch) TV late at night.
   i) I got _____ (read) my e-mails every half hour.
   j) She got _____ (have) lunch at 12 o'clock every day.

6. Complete with *such, so, too* or *enough*:
   a) It's _____ cold to go outside.
   b) Joe isn't old _____ to vote.
   c) He's not strong _____ to lift the suitcase.
   d) She's _____ young to go out alone.
   e) The new car is _____ modern. I enjoy driving it.
   f) This is _____ a nice hotel. It's very conveniently located.
   g) They are _____ intelligent kids. They always get A in the tests.
   h) The new TV program is _____ funny. We had a lot of fun last night watching it.
   i) It's _____ early to go to the party now. It only starts at 9 p.m.
   j) They were _____ worried with the plane delay, but everything went all right.
   k) They won't have _____ time to finish the article. It's due tomorrow.
   l) Last night we watched _____ an interesting movie. It was a new release.

> É importante prestar atenção em alguns tipos diferentes de uso de *so* e *such*.
>
> Dizemos:
> » *so long*, mas *such a long time*;
> » *so far*, mas *such a long way*;
> » *so many, so much*, mas *such a lot (of)*.
>
> Vejamos alguns exemplos:
> » I haven't seen him for so long (or such a long time) that I've forgotten what he looks like.
> » I didn't know you lived so far (or such a long way) from the city.
> » Why did you buy so much (or such a lot of) food?

Exercise Approaching Collocations

7. Match the first column with the second to make proper collocations:
   a) business   ( ) traditions
   b) foreign   ( ) trip
   c) various   ( ) to declare
   d) exchange   ( ) country
   e) cash   ( ) time
   f) make   ( ) appointments
   g) booking   ( ) flights and hotels
   h) local   ( ) rate
   i) goods   ( ) advance
   j) business   ( ) presentations

Síntese do capítulo

No presente capítulo, abordamos três pontos gramaticais importantes no aprendizado da língua inglesa. O primeiro refere-se a como expressamos hábitos e atitudes que se repetiam no passado e que não acontecem mais no presente. O segundo diz respeito a ações com as quais estamos acostumados. O terceiro refere-se a algumas expressões, ou *function words*, usadas no singular e no plural com a função de intensificar adjetivos e substantivos. Além desses pontos, apresentamos dois textos sobre organização de viagens de negócios, com informações relevantes para o profissional que precisa fazer viagens nacionais ou internacionais. Por último, sugerimos exercícios de fixação com o objetivo de contribuir para a revisão dos tópicos desenvolvidos neste capítulo.

O hotel/The hotel

Fazer uma reserva em um hotel é uma experiência pela qual todos passamos, regularmente ou, pelo menos, algumas vezes na vida. Para os que precisam viajar a trabalho, reservar um hotel vem a ser uma tarefa quase rotineira. Por isso, seguem algumas sugestões sobre como cumprir essa tarefa de maneira rápida e eficiente.

Certamente, nos dias atuais, a forma mais frequente para efetuar uma reserva é por *e-mail*.

Writing an e-mail

A single bedroom reservation

From: Mrs. Brown
To: Reservation Department of Mercury Hotel/London
Date: 19 October 2009
Reference: A single bedroom reservation

Dear Sir/Madam,

I am writing to make a reservation of a single bedroom from November 26th to November 29th, 2009, in my name, Mrs. Sarah Brown, general manager of KLB Enterprises.

My flight is due to arrive at 6:45 a.m., so I would like to request an early check in and also a late check out, as the flight departure time is 8:00 p. m.

Our company has chosen this hotel due to all the facilities provided to the guests, such as, wireless for Internet and special meals for vegetarians. We do hope both facilities will be available, as mentioned above.

The payment will be done by bank transfer, so I would be grateful if you could send me the bank information for transfer purpose as soon as possible.

Should you have any questions, please feel free to send me an e-mail, which will be answered immediately.

Thank you for your attention.

Yours faithfully,

Sarah Brown (Mrs)

KLB General Manager

Exercise

1. What is the purpose of the e-mail?
   a) To cancel a reservation.
   b) To make a reservation.
   c) To ask for information.
   d) To require Internet facilities.
   e) To require vegetarian meals.

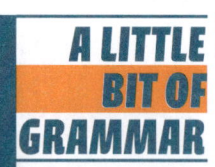

A LITTLE BIT OF GRAMMAR

Relative pronouns

Relative pronouns are very important because they enable us to make longer and more elaborated sentences. However, certain points must be taken into account. The first point to be considered is who or what the pronoun refers to, that is to say:

» When the pronoun refers to a **person**.
» When the pronoun refers to a **thing**.

Let's look at the following example:

» Sarah Brown is the person **who** has written the e-mail above.
   › The relative pronoun *who* refers to Sarah Brown, a person.

» Should you have any questions, please feel free to send me an e-mail, **which** will be answered immediately.
   › The relative pronoun *which* refers to the e-mail, a thing.

Another important point to consider is related to the subject or the object of the sentence. When the pronoun is related to subject and this subject is a person, who or that may be used.

» Sarah is the person **who**/**that** has written the e-mail.
   › The pronouns *who* and *that* refer to the person (subject/ person).

When the pronoun is related to an object and this object is a person, *who* or *that* may be used.

» I want to know the boss **who**/**that** the technician talked about.
   › The pronouns *who* and *that* refer to the boss (object/ person).

When the pronoun is related to a subject or an object, and this subject or object is a thing, *which* or *that* may be used.

» The e-mail, **which**/**that** has just arrived, is about a reservation.
   › The pronouns *which* and *that* refer to the e-mail (subject/ thing).

» Typing is something **which**/**that** I love.
   › The pronouns *which* and *that* refer to something (object/ thing).

The relative pronoun whom is more usual in formal language, but we have to use it when we are referring to a person and there is a preposition before the pronoun.

» To **whom** it may concern. (*A quem possa interessar*)

Chart 9.1 – Relative pronouns

Function in the sentence	People	Things
Subject	who, that	which, that
Object	whom, who, that	which, that

There is another relative pronoun, which can be used for a person and for a thing and refers to possession: *whose*.

» The accountant, **whose** e-mail I read, is my friend.
» The hotel, **whose** bedroom the general manager reserved, is five stars.

Exercises

2. Write sentences with relative pronouns following the pattern given:

Pattern A: The man **who** works for the main newspaper is a friend of mine.
a) journalist/write/those interesting articles/friend/hers.

b) fashion designer/design/last fashion show/cousin/ours.

c) professor/give/computer science course/colleague/theirs.

Pattern B: The office **which** they moved to is very modern.
a) report/read/quite interesting.

b) computer /buy/very fast.

c) lecture/attend/rather boring.

Pattern C: Mr. Smith, **whose** companies are all top technology, doesn't like publicity.
a) Mrs. Brown/husband/general manager/to be on the spotlight.

b) Mr. Green/employees/very loyal/to expand business.

c) Mrs. Gray/secretary/very efficient/to work on Saturdays.
_____

3. Complete the sentences with a relative pronoun:
   a) The knife,_____ we used to cut the meat with, is very sharp.
   b) The man to_____ I gave the book is a friend of mine.
   c) The London train,_____ should arrive at 7 o'clock, is late.
   d) Bernard Shaw,_____ had a long beard, was a very clever writer.
   e) The employer,_____ I dislike, works in the next room.
   f) Shakespeare,_____ is the world's greatest writer, was born in a little cottage.
   g) Tom and Mary,_____ are playing in the garden, are very naughty children.
   h) Beethoven,_____ music you've been listening to, was one of the world's finest composer.
   i) He met my mother from_____ he got the news of my divorce.
   j) The teacher in the next class,_____ name I can't remember, makes a lot of mistakes.

4. Join the sentences with a relative pronoun:
   a) The man is a gardener. He is watering the plants.
   _____

   b) The girl is a brilliant student. Her father is my assistant.
   _____

   c) The woman will start tomorrow. He hired her yesterday.
   _____

   d) My young sister has just graduated. You met her at my office last week.
   _____

   e) My boss is not very kind to me. I have worked for him for 2 months.
   _____

   f) What is the name of the director? She came here last night.
   _____

   g) Swimming makes people strong. It is a good sport.
   _____

A LITTLE BIT OF READING

Travel wisely, travel well

There are a few simple rules about how to make life easier, both before and after your journey. First of all, it is very important to check and double check departure times.

Once, I arrived at the airport a few minutes after ten. My secretary had got the ticket for me and I thought she had said that the plane left at 10:50 a.m. I walked calmly to the departure desk, thinking that I still had some time to spare. I hadn't bothered to take a look at the ticket. The clerk at the desk told me politely but firmly that the departure time was 10:15 and that the flight was, according to international regulations, "now closed". I had to wait for three hours for the next one and missed an important meeting.

Another point to remember concerns the weather at someone's final destination, otherwise one may arrive, for instance, in Rome, where it is not so cold in May, with loads of coats. In fact, some light clothes might be much more suitable for this time of the year.

Source: Adaptado de O'Neill, 2005.

Exercise

5. Complete the sentences with the suitable word, according to the passage:
   a) The writer of the passage _____ the plane. (lost/boarded/missed/changed/got on)
   b) The writer _____ the time of the flight. (understood/misunderstood/forgot/asked/changed)
   c) It is a good idea to take _____ to Rome in May. (winter clothes/summer clothes/swimming clothes/smart clothes/casual clothes)

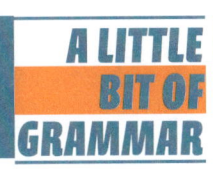

A LITTLE BIT OF GRAMMAR

Past Perfect, the use of *yet*, *just* and *already*

The *Past Perfect* tense is formed with the auxiliary verb *to have*, in the Simple Past, and the Past Participle of the main verb. In other words, by placing *had* ('d) before the Past Participle of the main verb.

The Past Perfect tense describes an action which took place before a definite time in the past, so it is often used with another verb in the Simple Past.

Let's observe these examples:

» When Mary **arrived**, Peter **wrote** the e-mail. (Simple Past/Simple Past)

The sentence above gives the idea that Peter didn't start writing the e-mail before Mary arrived, that is to say, maybe he was waiting for Mary to arrive before he started writing the e-mail.

» When Mary **arrived**, Peter **was writing** the e-mail. (Simple Past/Past Continuous)

The sentence above shows that Peter was in the middle of an action, writing an e-mail, when Mary arrived, so he didn't wait for Mary to arrive.

» When Mary **arrived**, Peter **had** already (or just) **written** the e-mail. (Simple Past/Past Perfect)

The sentence above shows that Peter did the action of writing the e-mail first, that is, before Mary arrived. In other words, in the sentence above, there are two actions in the past, but whoever reads or listens to this sentence understands that one action took place before the other:
› First action: Peter had already/just written the e-mail.
› Second action: Mary arrived.

It is important to emphasize that, in negative sentences, we usually use the adverb *yet* with the Past Perfect.

» When Mary arrived, Peter had not (hadn't) written the e-mail **yet**. (Simple Past/Past Perfect negative)

Exercises

6. Follow the example to answer the questions:

Jane: Were you in time to stop the sales rep. sending the e-mail?
John: No, when I arrived she'd just sent it.

a) **Jane**: Were you in time to stop the sales rep. throwing the garbage away?

___

b) **Jane**: Were you in time to stop the sales rep. reading the confidential letter?

___

c) **Jane**: Were you in time to stop the sales rep. going away?
_____

7. Now let's do the same exercise, but answering the question using the adverb *yet*:

   Jane: Were you in time to stop the sales rep. sending the e-mail?
   John: Yes, when I arrived, she hadn't sent it yet.

   a) **Jane**: Were you in time to stop the sales rep. throwing the garbage away?
   _____

   b) **Jane**: Were you in time to stop the sales rep. reading the confidential letter?
   _____

   c) **Jane**: Were you in time to stop the sales rep. going away?
   _____

8. Let's join the sentences using the connective *because* and the Simple Past/Past Perfect. Look at the example:

   He worked hard in the morning. He felt tired in the afternoon.
   He felt tired in the afternoon because he had worked hard in the morning.

   a) Paul arrived late at work. He missed the bus.
   _____

   b) George won the prize. He celebrated his victory with his coworkers.
   _____

   c) They left the door unlocked. A thief got into the company.
   _____

   d) He didn't answer all the questions. He wasn't hired.
   _____

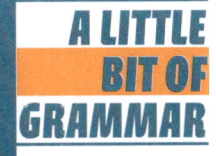

A LITTLE BIT OF GRAMMAR

The pronouns *where*, *when*, *why*

Os pronomes a seguir não são pronomes relativos, mas podem ser usados de maneira similar quando se referem a:

» Lugar – **Where**
  › Rio de Janeiro is the city where the headquarters is located.

» Tempo – **When**
  › Early in the morning is the time when I usually meet my boss.

» Motivo – **Why**
  › The reason why the reservation was canceled should be written in the e-mail.

Os verbos *miss* e *lose* (*lost*, no *Simple Past*) significam "perder", mas usamos o verbo *lose* quando perdemos o que nos pertence (exemplo: *I lost my keys*). O verbo *miss*, porém, pode ser usado como "perder o que não nos pertence" (exemplo: *I missed the bus, the lesson*); como "faltar" (exemplo: *Who missed the class yesterday?*); e como "sentir saudade" (exemplo: *I miss you*).

Exercise Approaching Collocations

9. Complete the text with the suitable expression:

| as soon as possible | facilities provided | departure times | late checkout | time to spare |
| single bedroom | points to remember | makes a reservation | due to arrive | early checkin |

When John has to travel, he usually (a) _____ on the Internet. Most of the times, he travels alone, so he books a (b) _____. Many times, he arrives early and departs late due to his many commitments. For this reason, he often asks for an (c) _____ and a (d) _____. When John is (e) _____ at the airport, he makes sure he has checked all his (f) _____ and that he has plenty of (g) _____ not to miss his flights. (h) _____, when he arrives at his destination, he verifies if the hotel really offers all the (i) _____ on the e-mail confirmation. These are very important (j) _____, when traveling anywhere.

Síntese do capítulo

Neste capítulo, vimos como podemos nos comunicar de modo mais funcional e elaborado por meio do uso de pronomes relativos. Além disso, abordamos o *Past Perfect*, tempo verbal que também possibilita uma comunicação mais clara entre o leitor e o escritor e/ou entre o falante e o ouvinte, no que diz respeito à cronologia de fatos ou eventos do passado.

Reuniões, conferências e palestras

10

O relatório tem um papel importante em qualquer tipo de empresa ou escritório. Escrevemos relatórios por diversas razões: para comunicar ideias e resultados decorrentes de pesquisas ou para relatar acontecimentos importantes no ambiente de trabalho. A seguir, apresentamos um texto com os vários pontos que um relatório deve conter.

A LITTLE BIT OF READING

Writing a report

First of all, let's see a very simple definition of a report and the reasons to write one: it is usually an official document, after the subject has been considered or investigated. People usually write it to give a spoken or **written** account of something that has been observed, done or investigated.

In this chapter we will restrict the information to written reports only.

A report can cover a wide range of subjects and should be written in an accurate, objective and complete way. It should have a clear purpose and a specific audience. Below, you find parts of good report writing:

Introduction
- » The aim of this report is to...
- » It is based on...
- » This report is intended to...
- » It draws on...
- » This report looks at/describes...
- » It uses...

Report an observation
- It seems/appears that...
- It was found that...

Observation
- ...tend(s) to (do)...
- It was felt that...
- A/The majority/minority of...
- ...were in the majority /minority

Quoting
- According to...
- As he said...
- In the words of...

Speculating
- It may/could/might (well) be that....may/could/might + (do/ have done)

Generalizing
- In general...
- On the whole...

Commenting
- Interestingly...
- Curiously...
- Oddly...
- Strangely...
- Surprisingly...
- Predictably...
- As might be (have been) expected...
- It is interesting that...

Making a recommendation
- It is recommended that...
- (Perhaps) It is/would be advisable for to (do)
- (Perhaps) X might/should consider + ing

Summing up
- To sum up
- To summarise
- On balance
- In short

Source: Adaptado de Unilearning, 2012a.

Exercise

1. Leia o texto novamente e responda às seguintes perguntas:
   a) Why is a report written?
   b) Give some suggestions of the possible divisions a report may have.
   c) What can you write a report about?
   d) How should a report be written?

Below, you find an example of a good executive report.

A LITTLE BIT OF READING

The aim of this report is to provide an analysis and evaluation of the current and prospective profitability, liquidity and financial stability of Outdoor Equipment Ltd. Methods of analysis include *trend*, *horizontal* and *vertical* analyses, as well as *ratios* such as Debt, Current and Quick ratios. Other calculations include rates of return on Shareholders Equity and Total Assets and earnings per share to name a few. All calculations can be found in the appendices. Results of data analyzed show that all ratios are below industry averages. In particular, comparative performance is poor in the areas of profit margins, liquidity, credit control, and inventory management.

It was found that the prospects of the company in its current position are not positive. The major areas of weakness require further investigation and remedial action by management. Recommendations discussed include:
» Improving the average collection period for accounts receivable.
» Improving/increasing inventory turnover.
» Reducing prepayments and perhaps increasing inventory levels.

The report also investigates the fact that the analysis conducted has limitations. Interestingly, some of the limitations include: forecasting figures are not provided; nature and type of company is not known; nor the current economic conditions data limitations, as not enough information is provided or enough detail, i.e. monthly details not known; results are based on past performances, not present.

Source: Adaptado de Unilearning, 2012b.

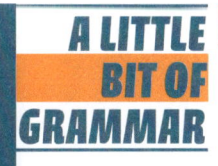

A LITTLE BIT OF GRAMMAR

Passive voice (*Voz passiva*)

The passive voice is used when we want to focus on the action, not on whom or what is performing this action, so that the object is more important than the subject. That is why it is very frequent in newspaper communication.

For instance:

» **President Kennedy was assassinated in Texas.** (Who did the action is not important).

Also, the passive voice can be more polite sometimes, as in the example that follows:

- **A mistake was made**. (Here, the focus is on the mistake and not on who made it, which is not important).

How to form it

The passive voice is formed with the auxiliary verb *to be* in many different tenses, according to the time of the action and the Past Participle of the main verb. It is used as the following:

- Passive voice in the Present (verb *to be* in the Present).
  - The manager **is taken** to the airport whenever he flies to visit the branches.
- Passive voice in the Past (verb *to be* in the Past).
  - The manager **was taken** to the airport last week.
- Passive voice in the Present Continuous (verb *to be* in the Present Continuous)
  - The manager is **being taken** to the airport.
- Passive voice in the Past Continuous (verb *to be* in the Past Continuous).
  - When the accident happened, the manager **was being taken** to the airport.
- Passive voice in the Future (verb *to be* in the Future).
  - The manager **is going to be taken** to the airport tomorrow.
  - The manager **will be taken** to the airport tomorrow.
- Passive voice in the Present Perfect (verb *to be* in the Present Perfect).
  - The manager **has** already **been taken** to the airport.
- Passive voice in the Past Perfect (verb *to be* in the Past Perfect).
  - When I arrived, the manager **had** already **been taken** to the airport.
- Passive voice in the Conditional (verb *to be* in the Conditional).
  - If the secretary made all the arrangements, the manager **would be taken** to the airport.
- Passive voice with modal verbs (verb *to be* used with a modal verb).
  - The information about the purchase **may be given** to the customer by e-mail.
  - The information about the purchase **could be given** to the customer by e-mail.
  - The information about the purchase **should be given** to the customer by e-mail.

> The information about the purchase **must be given** to the customer by e-mail.
> The information about the purchase **ought to be given** to the customer by e-mail.
> The information about the purchase **needs to be given** to the customer by e-mail.

When to use it

The passive voice is used in the following basic situations:

» When the agent of the action is unknown or is not important.
> The manager **has** already **been taken** to the airport.

» To emphasize the object (receiver) of the action.
> Mary **was given** the prize as the best employee in the company.

» To make generic statements, announcements, and explanations.
> Customers **are asked** not to smoke inside the company.

Exercises

2. Write sentences in the passive voice following the pattern given:

Pattern A: The documents he carries **are** always **photocopied**.

a) car/drive/usually/rent

_____

b) computer/use/often/hire

_____

c) houses/build/always/sell

_____

d) articles/write/seldom/publish

_____

Pattern B: The answer **was not known**.

e) question /understand

_____

f) witness /believe

_____

g) letters/post

_____

h) story/remember

_____

Pattern C: The (secretary) has not been trained yet[1].

i) flight/already/authorize
_____

j) repair/just/complete
_____

k) money/always /deposit
_____

l) cheque/never /cash
_____

Pattern D: The film **will be shown** next week.

m) machine/test/next month
_____

n) product launch/in March
_____

o) cattle/auction/at Easter
_____

p) paintings/exhibit/next week
_____

3. Match the parts to form a complete sentence:

   a) Competition! 5.000 prizes…   ( ) …has been disconnected.
   b) Five people…   ( ) …will be sent to the winners.
   c) The telephone…   ( ) …should be received by e-mail.
   d) When I checked, the phone bill…   ( ) …were killed in the explosion.
   e) Further information…   ( ) …is not permitted in the station.
   f) Before the storm everyone…   ( ) …had not been paid.
   g) Smoking…   ( ) …is currently being rebuilt.
   h) The old town theatre…   ( ) …was told to stay inside home.

Conectivos (*connectives*)

Os conectivos são palavras que ajudam a ligar frases e sentenças e que possibilitam uma maior fluidez na língua escrita e falada. Para tanto, geralmente, usamos as conjunções e os advérbios.

As conjunções são divididas nas seguintes classes[2]:

» **Coordinating conjunctions** – *And, but, or, nor, so*.

---

[1] When we take the adverb *yet* out and replace it by *already*, *just*, *always* and *never*, we should remember that the latter ones are used before the main verb.

[2] Adaptado de MacFadyen, 2012.

› Essas conjunções ligam palavras individuais, frases e orações independentes. *But* e *for* também podem ser usadas como preposições.
  › He likes to write e-mails **and** reports.
  › They like to use computers **but** they don't like to use the fax machine.
  › We like to attend lectures **or** workshops during congresses.
  › Mary isn't an efficient secretary; **nor** is Jane.
  › It was going to rain **so** I took my umbrella.

» **Subordinating conjunctions** – *After, although, as, because, before, how, if, once, since, than, that, though, until (till), when, where, whether, while.*
  › Essas conjunções introduzem uma oração dependente e indicam o tipo de relação entre as orações dependentes e independentes.
    › **After** she got a car, she felt more independent.
    › **Although** it was raining hard, they went out.
    › The phone rang **as** the secretary was leaving.
    › She didn't buy the printer **because** it was very expensive.
    › **Before** going out, they turned off all the computers.
    › They don't know **how** the problem was solved.
    › **If** you need any help, please give us a call.
    › **Once** they left the company, everything got resolved.
    › She has been much better, **since** she went to see the doctor.
    › Mary has a better car **than** her assistant.
    › It used to be **that** the winter was much colder.
    › We see him every day. We've never spoken to him **though**.
    › Let's wait **until** (**till**) it stops raining to go out.
    › Call our branch **when** you arrive in Melbourne.
    › John doesn't know **where** he left his office keys.
    › We aren't sure **whether** we should go or not.
    › You should wait **while** I make a phone call.

» **Correlative conjunctions** – *Both... and, either... or, neither... nor, not only... but also, so... as, whether... or.*
  › Essas conjunções geralmente aparecem em pares e são usadas para ligar elementos equivalentes dentro das sentenças. Tecnicamente, as conjunções correlativas são, simplesmente, a conjunção coordenativa ligada a um adjetivo ou advérbio.
    › He **both** sells **and** buys the goods.
    › We can **either** go to the canteen **or** to the company restaurant.
    › They **neither** came **nor** called us.
    › **Not only** did she finish the job, **but also** got a raise.
    › She is **so** efficient **as** the last secretary.
    › He doesn't care **whether** he stays here **or** moves to Chicago.

Exercise

4. Choose the best conjunction to join the sentences:
   a) I lived in London. I left college. (if, although, until)
   _____

   b) They'll be happy. This job is finished. (when, or, while)
   _____

   c) He'd like to see you. You leave the office. (before, and, although)
   _____

   d) Ann made coffee. Bill toasted the bread. (if, while, when)
   _____

   e) She speaks Chinese, Japanese. (both... and)
   _____

A LITTLE BIT OF READING

What is videoconferencing?

Videoconferencing is a communication technology that integrates video and voice to connect remote users with each other as if they were in the same room. It is necessary to have a computer, webcam, microphone, and broadband Internet connection for video conferences. People can see and hear each other in real time, which allows natural conversations with an up-to-date communication technology.

It has become very important to the business sector, as videoconferences allow users to save time and money, since they do not need to leave their place of business and may talk to people face-to-face on virtual time.

The list of advantages from using videoconferencing is long, and here are a few of the main ones, like the enormous savings on traveling for companies and business people. Companies may have more people at a meeting and save much more. With videoconferences, a half day presentation is, many times, enough and the executives may spend the rest of the time they would be traveling, doing productive work in their offices.

It also makes it easier for businesses to access outside experts, in order to compare notes and pool together their findings to accelerate the process of problem solving. Sometimes, the meeting will be in the company's office and a small lecture or training talk is all that is necessary.

Source. Adaptado de Wiseyeek, 2012; Gorman, 2006.

Exercises

5. Complete the text with the conjunctions from the box:

   although although and and and so
   because because before when until

   Andy Brown didn't like school, (a) _____ he left (b) _____ he was seventeen years old (c) _____ got a job at the airport. He stayed there a short time, (d) _____ he liked the work. He decided to leave (e) _____ the pay was very low (f) _____ he had to work long hours. His next job was in an import-export company. He liked that much more, (g) _____ he traveled abroad a lot (h) _____ the salary was much better. He worked there for four years, (i) _____ he really knew the business well; then he started his own company. Now he is doing very well, (j) _____ he, sometimes, works very hard. He wants to make enough money to stop working (k) _____ he is 50.

6. Write AV if the sentence is in the active voice or PV if the sentence is in the passive voice:
   a) (   ) Someone will read you the other part of the instructions.
   b) (   ) Let me know if there is something we should do.
   c) (   ) Haven't the products been paid yet?
   d) (   ) Rough paper must not be thrown away.
   e) (   ) Employees are not allowed to smoke in the restrooms.

7. Change the sentences from active to passive voice starting with the highlighted words. Sometimes a preposition may be included:
   a) The customer asked the company for **a new contract**.
   _____

   b) When we first met, they had already offered Mary **the job at the bank**.
   _____

   c) The company will give Mr. Jackson **a notice of dismissal**.
   _____

   d) His employer has assigned Mr. Green **too many duties**.
   _____

   e) The bank is lending Mr. Smith **the money**.
   _____

Destacamos a importância e a recorrência do uso da voz passiva em linguagem jornalística.

- » Two people were killed and five injured in a car crash yesterday...
- » The criminal will be arrested, judged and probably executed soon...
- » A thousand employees have been sacked due to the great recession...
- » What to wear when traveling.

É frequente também, nesse tipo de linguagem, como vemos nos exemplos anteriores, o uso do verbo auxiliar *to be* apenas uma vez.

Dificuldades especiais

Many times a verb has two objects. In this case, it is possible to write the sentence using two kinds of passive voice, each one starting with a different object.

- » The employees gave flowers to the boss.
    - › Subject: the employees
    - › Verb: gave (in the Simple Past: give – gave – given)
    - › Object one: flowers
    - › Object two: the boss

So:
- » **Flowers were given** to the boss by the employees.

Or:
- » **The boss was given** flowers by the employees.

Exercises Approaching Collocations

8. Match the words on the right with the ones on the left.

a) written ( ) experts
b) official ( ) account
c) clear ( ) sector
d) specific ( ) document
e) make ( ) connection
f) communication ( ) purpose
g) video ( ) conference
h) Internet ( ) audience
i) business ( ) technology
j) outside ( ) a recommendation

9. Now complete the sentences below with one of the expressions from the previous exercise:
   a) The board made sure that the _____ was sent to headquarters.
   b) The _____ is always very important to be checked later on.
   c) Since representatives at the meeting had not a _____ for the final decision a new date was set up for next month.
   d) The _____ was a very important part for the decision taken by the board.
   e) All the ones present were asked to _____ to be sent to the CEO.
   f) The vice president was asked to contract _____ for the next board meeting.
   g) A sales committee was formed, but not all the representatives from the new _____ were present to sign the official form.
   h) They had problems with the _____, so the meeting had to be postponed.
   i) After much discussion about the new _____ they agreed on the new server.
   j) The vice president made sure a very _____ was present at the conference, so they would only discuss what was on the agenda.

Síntese do capítulo

No presente capítulo, abordamos todos os tempos verbais na voz passiva. Enfatizamos a importância do uso de tais estruturas e apresentamos textos para exercitar a leitura, bem como vários exercícios gramaticais que possibilitarão uma melhor compreensão a respeito dos assuntos tratados. Outra matéria complexa abordada neste capítulo foi o uso de conjunções, que servem para ligar palavras, frases e sentenças. O emprego do conectivo adequado contribui para a coesão e a coerência do texto, ou seja, a conjunção certa para cada frase faz com que o sentido seja mais bem compreendido.

Apresentando-se em uma entrevista

Considerando o velho provérbio popular "A primeira impressão é a que fica", acreditamos que um candidato a uma vaga de emprego deve tomar muito cuidado ao se apresentar em uma entrevista na empresa.

A LITTLE BIT OF READING

Having a job interview

Step 1

Learn as much as you can about the company you would like to work for. Get information from your friends, relatives, teachers etc. This way, you will be able to feel comfortable and confident to answer any kind of question the interviewer may ask you concerning the prospective job.

Step 2

Think carefully about which clothes to wear on this important day. Dress to impress, but be professional and have a traditional and conservative appearance which may open doors for you.

Step 3

Be confident! Being confident means trusting yourself, so give a firm hand shake, have a positive attitude, a friendly smile, and keep eye contact.

Step 4

There are always questions to be answered, so think about what to say if you are asked questions like:

» Why did you leave your last job? (if any)
» What are you very good at?
» What are your objectives?
» How can you contribute to the growth of our organization?

Step 5
Remember it is a job interview. Do not give irrelevant information. Keep to the point and be concise, but try not to be laconic so as not to give the impression you are in a bad mood.

Source: Adaptado de Ehow, 2011.

Exercise

1. Agora, vamos investigar os detalhes do texto. Which step mentions:
   a) How to greet the interviewer.

   b) Search for information about the company in advance.

   c) Avoid extra conversation.

   d) Wear suitable clothes for the interview.

   e) Be confident.

   f) Think about answers to possible asked questions.

   g) Be in a good mood.

   h) Search for information about the interviewer in advance.

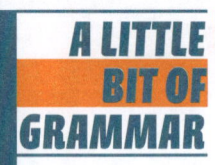

A LITTLE BIT OF GRAMMAR

Discurso direto e indireto

Uma conversa ou um discurso podem ser diretos ou indiretos. Denominamos *discurso direto* (*direct speech*) a transmissão das exatas palavras do emissor. Ao escrevê-las, usamos aspas.

» "I'm really tired", Jane said.

Quando contamos a outras pessoas, com nossas palavras, o que foi dito por alguém, usamos o chamado *discurso indireto* (*indirect*, or *reported speech*):

» Jane said (that) she was really tired.

Quando usamos o discurso indireto, geralmente estamos nos referindo a acontecimentos no passado. Sendo assim, todas as sentenças são reportadas com um tempo verbal relacionado ao passado.

> Nesse caso, o uso do pronome relativo **that** é opcional.

Observe, no Chart 11.1, alguns exemplos de uso dos tempos verbais para o discurso indireto.

Chart 11.1 – Usos de tempos verbais para o discurso indireto

Tempos verbais	Exemplos
Imperative to Infinitive	"**Wait** for me." I told him **to wait** for me. "Please **wait**!" I asked him **to wait**.
Simple Present to Simple Past	"She **needs** some help." She said (that) she **needed** some help.
Present Continuous to Past Continuous	"They **are having** a meeting." She said (that) they **were having** a meeting.
Present Perfect to Past Perfect	"We **have been** to that company." You said (that) we **had been** to that company.
Future to Conditional	"I **will be** home at 8:00." He said (that) he **would be** home at 8:00.
Past Simple to Past Perfect	"You **wrote** an article to the paper." I said (that) you **had written** an article to the paper.
Be going to to *was/were going to*	"They **are going to** call us later." I said (that) they **were going to** call us later.
Must	"You **must turn in** the paper today." I said (that) you **had to turn in** the paper that day.

Outro aspecto que deve ser considerado quando se faz a passagem do discurso direto para o discurso indireto refere-se à necessidade de modificar também algumas expressões de tempo.

Para melhor compreender o que queremos dizer, veja o Chart 11.2:

Chart 11.2 – Expressões de tempo a serem modificadas

Discurso direto	Discurso indireto
tonight	that night
today	that day
this week/month/year	that week/month/year
yesterday	the day before/the previous day
last night/week/month/year	the night/week/month/year before/the previous night/week/month/year
tomorrow	the day after/the following/next day
next week/month/year	the next/following week/month/year
two days/weeks/months/years ago	two days/weeks/months/years before
this/these	that/those
here	there
come	go
now	then

> **Partícula *if* no discurso indireto**
> no discurso indireto, usamos a partícula *if* em sentenças interrogativas que requerem respostas simples (afirmativas ou negativas). Vejamos alguns exemplos:
> » Is the bus stop here?
> › She asked me **if** the bus stop was here (there).
> » Do they have extra tickets for the theatre?
> › I asked him **if** they had extra tickets for the theatre.

Há verbos que são facilmente confundidos: *say, tell, speak, ask*. Veja alguns exemplos:
› ***Say*** something. (dizer algo)
› ***Tell*** somebody something. (dizer algo para alguém)
› ***Tell*** somebody to do something. (mandar alguém fazer algo)
› ***Ask*** somebody to do something. (pedir a alguém para fazer algo)

» *Speak* descreve o ato de falar.
› Sam **spoke** to us in the office yesterday.

» *Say* descreve as palavras usadas. Pode ser seguido por *that* no discurso indireto.
› "It's hot today", she **said**. / She said (*that*) it was hot.

» *Tell* descreve o ato de dar informação. Necessita de um objeto e pode ser seguido por *that* no discurso indireto.
› "You've won the prize", he said. / He **told me** (*that*) I had won the prize.

Exercises

2. Rewrite each sentence in reported speech, beginning as shown:

    "Are you staying at the new branch all summer?", the manager asked me.
    The manager asked me <u>if I was staying at the new branch all summer.</u>

    a) "Have you done your work?", I asked the assistant.
       I asked the assistant _____.
    b) "Did you remember to lock the drawer?", the boss asked him.
       His boss asked him _____.
    c) "Do they speak Chinese?", the waiter asked the tour guide.
       The waiter asked the tour guide _____.
    d) "Have they finished their tasks at work?", the manager asked the secretary.
       The manager asked the secretary _____.

3. Complete each sentence using the verbs *say, tell* or *speak* in an appropriate form:

   Example:
   Ben told me that he was playing soccer on Sundays.
   a) She _____ her friends about the party, and they _____ they would come.
   b) Our teacher _____ us not to _____ anything during the lecture.
   c) I _____ to my friends that I _____ Chinese, but they didn't believe me.
   d) He _____ to Sarah, and she _____ she would call Diane.

4. Choose the correct sentence:
   a) ( ) I said the driver I wanted to go to the airport.
      ( ) I told the driver I wanted to go to the airport.
   b) ( ) My father said there was a letter for me from the company I had sent my CV to.
      ( ) My father told there was a letter for me from the company I had sent my CV to.
   c) ( ) Everybody said it was a great company to work for.
      ( ) Everybody told it was a great company to work for.
   d) ( ) Sally spoke she was making a phone call.
      ( ) Sally said she was making a phone call.
   e) ( ) John said Peter to close the door.
      ( ) John asked Peter to close the door.
   f) ( ) His mother said him to call his boss.
      ( ) His mother told him to call his boss.
   g) ( ) She spoke the technician about the big problem they were having with the new computers.
      ( ) She told the technician about the big problem they were having with the new computers.
   h) ( ) Sue asked the sales team to give her a return on their sales.
      ( ) Sue said the sales team to give her a return on their sales.

5. Rewrite the following sentences into reported speech:
   a) "Are you going to work?", John asked.
   _____

   b) "Did you stay for the lecture?", Mary asked me.
   _____

   c) "Do you work here?", my friend asked Peter.
   _____

   d) "Have you been here before?", I asked Joan.
   _____

   e) "Stay a little longer!", Susan asked her friend.
   _____

Curiosidades

É interessante observar que, ao usarmos o discurso indireto com perguntas, a *wh question word* permanece. Como a pergunta já foi efetuada no começo da sentença (*Do you know...?*; *Can you tell me...?*), não se repete a forma interrogativa (usando auxiliares ou inversão) com os outros verbos. Para fazermos perguntas de uma maneira polida, podemos usar as expressões *Do you know* ou *Can you tell me*, mais a pergunta indireta.

- » Where does she live? / Do you know where she lives?
- » What does this word mean? / Do know you what this word means?
- » Where can we buy tickets? / Can you tell us where we can buy tickets?
- » How much does this cost? / Do you know how much this costs?
- » Which brother is older? / Can you tell me which brother is older?
- » Why are they leaving early? / Can you tell me why they are leaving early?

Os auxiliares *would*, *could*, *should*, *might*, *must* não sofrem nenhuma mudança no discurso indireto. Observe:

- » We would leave earlier if we could. / They said they would leave earlier if they could.
- » She could stay if you asked. / I said she could stay if you asked.
- » They should finish before leaving. / He said they should finish before leaving.
- » We might go to Europe in 2012. / We said we might go to Europe in 2012.

Note que esses auxiliares têm apenas uma forma, independentemente do discurso (direto ou indireto).

A LITTLE BIT OF READING

Writing a *Curriculum vitae* (CV)

Being able to write a *curriculum vitae* (CV) as well as an application or cover letter is extremely relevant, as it may mean the obtainment of a good job.

Having a latin origin, the word *curriculum* means the course of one's life, so we are expected to include in such document all the details about our lives. There are, certainly, many ways to write a CV, but let's have a look at the following example.

Peter Smith

☎ 0776868654 (M) 01707 273976 (H) 020 75773765 (W)
✉ 34 Crawford Road – Hatfield – Hertfordshire – AL10 0PE
peter.smith@gmail.com

Professional Experience

2001 – present | Bank of Tokyo [London]
Manager – Intel® Server Support Team
» Head of team (9 members), responsible for overall management of 150 staff.
» Strategic technical planning for Intel® environment.

12/1999 – 07/2001 | Bank of Scotland [Glasgow]
Senior NT/NetWare Specialist
» Member of Lan Server Group, responsible for 3rd support of company servers.
» "Business As Usual" administration and troubleshooting of Netware Servers.

01/1999 – 11/1999 | Lan Designers Association [Brazil]
Network Engineer/Consultant
» Consultancy role for small to medium businesses from conception to implementation and maintenance.
» Providing solutions for clients through companies' needs and requirements.

06/1998 – 12/1999 | TC Systems Consultants [Brazil]
Support Engineer
» Development of network solutions for Windows.
» Installation and configuration of networks TCP/IP and NETBeui.

1994 – 1998 | Freelance Analyst [Brazil]
» PC installations and repair.
» Hardware and Software – installation and configuration.

Qualifications
» MCP + INTERNET – Jun/06.
» MCP – Dec/05.
» MCSE – Jul/04.
» CNE Intranet ware 4.11 – Apr/04.
» CNA – Jul/04.

Languages
» Portuguese – written and spoken – fluent.

Concerning the application or cover letter, we should keep in mind the fact that it is, undoubtedly, as important as the CV, so let's also have a look at an example.

Cambridge – UK
AL10 0PE
Tel:02075773765
E-mail: mst@gmail.com
The Personnel Office
Intercontinental Hotel
43 Trafalgar Square
London – UK
15th January 2008

Dear Sir/Madam
I wish to apply for the post of manager, which was advertised in The Guardian Newspaper of February, 15th 2009.
As you can see from my CV enclosed, I believe I have the suitable qualifications and experience for the post.
Any further information may be provided, if necessary. So do not hesitate to contact me by telephone or e-mail.

Yours faithfully,
Peter Smith (Mr.)

Exercise Approaching Collocations

6. Choose the best word to complete the sentence:
   a) I'm writing to _____ of manager as advertised in the last issue of *The Economist Magazine*.
      ( ) appoint for the post
      ( ) apply for the post
      ( ) apply for the work
   b) At an interview, applicants should _____.
      ( ) feel happy
      ( ) fall confident
      ( ) feel confident
   c) If you are accepted, they will _____.
      ( ) contact you by phone
      ( ) find you by phone
      ( ) tell you by phone
   d) The new technician was hired to _____ for the computers.
      ( ) keep solutions
      ( ) maintain solutions
      ( ) provide solutions

e) She was very enthusiastic about the _____.
   ( ) prospective job
   ( ) useful job
   ( ) prospective idea
f) When being interviewed, applicants should always _____.
   ( ) maintain the point
   ( ) keep to the point
   ( ) respect the point
g) Secretaries are advised to _____ at important occasions.
   ( ) use formal clothes
   ( ) dress formal clothes
   ( ) wear formal clothes
h) When talking on the phone at the office, it's important to _____.
   ( ) be professional
   ( ) have professional
   ( ) keep professional
i) It's always possible to _____ about prospective customers on the internet.
   ( ) bring information
   ( ) take information
   ( ) find information
j) Speaking a foreign language usually _____ in many situations.
   ( ) close doors
   ( ) open doors
   ( ) slam doors

Síntese do capítulo

Neste capítulo, observamos um aspecto muito importante ao aprendermos uma língua estrangeira – o discurso indireto –, pois, no nosso dia a dia, constantemente contamos a alguém algo que ouvimos ou que nos foi dito. Assim, o aprendizado do uso correto do discurso indireto é essencial.

Correspondência empresarial 12

Neste último capítulo, vamos abordar o tema *correspondência*, assunto sobre o qual profissionais de diversas áreas devem se manter atualizados, pois, muitas vezes, têm de enviar cartas e *e-mails* em sua rotina de trabalho.

A carta empresarial deve ser escrita em uma linguagem precisa e formal. Esse tipo de correspondência costuma seguir um determinado modelo de apresentação, com um *layout* especial. Além disso, na redação utilizada em cartas empresariais, costuma-se fazer uso de expressões formais, a fim de garantir que o receptor não tenha problemas para compreender o conteúdo e para que possa, caso necessário, responder ao remetente sem dificuldades.

A seguir, vamos destacar os pontos mais importantes desse tipo de carta e visualizar alguns exemplos.

A LITTLE BIT OF READING

Writing formal letters

Formal letter writing should follow certain rules and criteria and be well written. Sometimes, it is a letter that will introduce a company or an executive. The fact that it is written in formal English shows respect and appreciation for the person or company receiving it. It should be as clear as possible, as well as concise.

Below there are some tips and rules on how a formal letter should be written. Remember, contractions should not be used in a formal letter.

1. Your address
    › The return address should be written on the top right hand corner of the letter, if you are not using paper with the company's letterhead.

2. The address of the person you are writing to
    › The addressee's address should be written on the left, starting below your address, including the person's or company's name.

3. Date
    › The date may be written on different sides of the page. It may be written either on the right or on the left of the line after the addressee. The month should be written as a word.

    March 29th, 2010.

4. Salutation or greeting
    Dear Sir/Madam,
    › Use these greetings if you do not know the name of the person you are writing to. However, you should always try to find out his/ her name.

    Dear Mr. Brown,
    › When you know the name, you should use the title (Mr., Mrs., Miss., Ms., Dr. etc.) and the last name only. When writing to a woman and it is not known if she uses Mrs. or Miss., you may use Ms., which is for married and single women.

5. Content – first paragraph
    › The first paragraph should be short and state the purpose of the letter. For instance:

    To make an enquiry.
    To complain.
    To request something.

6. The main text or the body of the letter
    › The paragraph or paragraphs following should contain the details or the necessary information. Letters in English should not be very long, keeping to the essentials and concentrating on organizing it in a clear and logical manner.

7. Last paragraph
    › The last paragraph of a formal letter should state what action you expect to be taken by the receiver, like: make a refund, send information requested, check on a bill or product received etc.

8. Ending a letter
    Yours faithfully
    › If you do not know the name of the person, end the letter this way.

Yours sincerely
› If you know the name of the person, end the letter this way.

Yours truly
Very truly yours
› You may end your letter like above if you are writing to someone in the United States.

9. Your signature
› Sign your name, then print it underneath the signature. If you think the person you are writing to might not know whether you are male of female, put your title in brackets after your name. Let's have a look at the following example[1].

Picture 12.1 – Example of a formal letter

(1) The New York Publishing Co.
123 East 78th Street
New York, n. Y. 10022
USA

Brentwood Book Store (2)
235 Main Street
Laguna Nigel, Ca. 17650 – USA
November 16th, 2009 (3)

Dear Mr. Brown,(4)

On October 15th, we sent you the invoice for your last order, which was due on November 1st. Up to now, we have not received any payment yet. As our company policy, we are sending you a reminder for the payment to be done ASAP. (5)

We understand you have received the last invoice, as you have requested another order to be sent by the end of the month. As you know, should we not receive any payment, it will not be possible to send the new one. (6)

In case you have already made the payment, please disregard this letter. We expect this matter to be all cleared and to continue doing business with your company.

If there are any questions, please do not hesitate to contact us. (7)

Yours sincerely, (8)

(your signature) (9)
Mary Smith (Mrs.)
Manager Accounts Receivable

Source: Adaptado de UE, 2012.

---

[1] Os números inseridos no corpo da carta relacionam-se com as explicações anteriores ao exemplo.

Abbreviations

It is also important to know some abbreviations used when writing a letter. Below, there is a list of the most important ones:

- **asap** = as soon as possible
- **cc** = carbon copy
    - When you send a copy of a letter to more than one person, you use this abbreviation to let them know.
- **enc**. = enclosure
    - When you include other papers with your letter.
- **pp** = *per procurationem*
    - A latin phrase meaning that you are signing the letter on somebody else's behalf (if they are not there to sign it themselves etc).
- **ps** = postscript
    - When you want to add something after you've finished and signed the letter.
- **pto** (informal) = please turn over (to make sure that the other person knows the letter continues on the other side of the page).
- **RSVP** = from the french *Réspondez S'il Vous Plaît*, meaning "please reply".

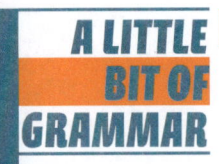

A LITTLE BIT OF GRAMMAR

Phrasal verbs

A phrasal verb is a verb followed by a preposition or an adverb. This combination of words enables the creation of a new word, which has quite a different meaning from the previous one. It is named phrasal verb, but in a sentence it may have the function of a verb or a noun.

Phrasal verbs are very common in spoken and written informal English, so we need them to understand and speak natural English.

- I **ran into** my manager at the movies last night.
    - run + into = meet

- The person who robbed the new branch escaped without leaving any trace. It was a clean **runaway**.
    - run + away = escape

There are some phrasal verbs which are made by an intransitive verb, that is, one which does not need an object.

- The new customer has just **rung up**.

Other phrasal verbs are transitive, so they will be followed by an object.

- The applicant **turned down** the offer.

Some transitive phrasal verbs must be separated. In this case, the object is situated between the verb and the preposition or adverb.

- I **talked** my boss **into** letting me take an extra day off.

Some transitive phrasal verbs may not be separated. The object must be placed after the preposition.

» I will **look for** the information the client asked me.

In some cases, it is possible to place the object either between the verb and the preposition or after the preposition.

» Please, **turn** the computer **on**.
» Please, **turn on** the computer.

Attention! When the object is a pronoun, rather than a noun, it must be placed between the verb and the preposition.

» Please, **turn** the computer **on**.
» Please, **turn on** the computer.
» Please, **turn** it **on**. ✓
» Please, **turn on** it. ✗

Exercise

1. Match the phrasal verb with its meaning:
   a) call off   ( ) to stop doing something
   b) check in   ( ) to cancel
   c) throw away   ( ) to connect/disconnect something from electricity
   d) fill out   ( ) to register at a hotel
   e) find out   ( ) to enter/leave a bus, car, train
   f) get on/off   ( ) to be something/somewhere in the end
   g) give up   ( ) to dispose of something
   h) turn into   ( ) to complete a form
   i) turn on/off   ( ) to dress
   j) put on   ( ) to discover

Dificuldades especiais[2]

Many foreign students know the most common phrasal verbs. However, the less frequent ones may be extremely difficult to understand. It is believed that the best way to learn them is to use them as much as possible in every day communication.

A LITTLE BIT OF READING

Give the perfect speech by using some easy steps

Speaking in front of a big crowd of people is intimidating, regardless if it's high school students or business executives. It is important to be

[2] Adaptado de Economics Network, 2012.

well prepared when one is going to give a speech. Usually, it is a formal occasion and it takes preparation, time and hard work.

Below, there are some steps which can help you give a perfect or near perfect speech.

» You should analyze your audience. You should consider the topic you are going to talk about, the audience's expectations, needs and objectives.
» The subject may vary and, sometimes, the speaker may not have a choice. If possible, choose an interesting topic and, based upon it, create a solid speech, which will make people listen to you.
» First of all, research about what you are going to talk about. Use facts and don't assume what the audience knows and consider the potential questions they may ask.
» The speaker should create an outline, using the thesis and the research done previously. Do not write out the speech completely. Base it upon your notes to speak freely.
» The speech should be practiced before a small audience, like family, friends, or even before a mirror.
» Analyze the strong and weak parts of the speech and verify the vocal fillers, body language and eye contact.
» Make a visual aid available, which is helpful for the audience to understand the topic better.
» The substance of a speech and to know what it is about is very important, but the way one dresses should not be left aside either. Choosing clothes that fit well with the audience, topic and overall environment gives the final touch for a perfect speech presentation.

Source: Adapted from Yahoo! Voices, 2012.

Exercises

2. In the text above, there are three phrasal verbs. Match them with their meanings:
   a) left aside   ( ) give assistance
   b) talk about   ( ) ignore
   c) help out   ( ) discuss something

3. Complete each sentence with one of the phrasal verbs below. Use each only once:

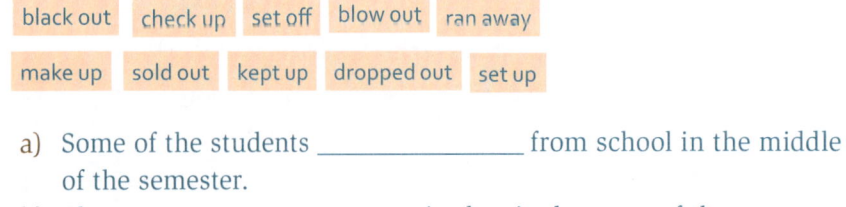

   black out   check up   set off   blow out   ran away
   make up   sold out   kept up   dropped out   set up

   a) Some of the students _____ from school in the middle of the semester.
   b) There was a _____ in the city because of the storm.

c) The children like when adults _____ stories; they are more interesting.
d) After the accident the driver didn't stay; he _____.
e) At the birthday party, the little girl loved when she had to _____ the candles.
f) The plane leaves in three hours. They should _____ for the airport now.
g) You should have a medical _____ every year.
h) The noise next door _____ me _____ until 3 a.m. I am very tired now.
i) The company was _____ to a big international enterprise.
j) They had to call a technician to _____ the computers after buying new ones.

Idiomatic expressions

Idioms are very frequent in any language because they add spice to the language. However, they may be quite hard for students of English to understand. Even if you have fluency in English and can make yourself clearly understood, how good is your knowledge of idiomatic phrases and expressions?

The English language has thousands of idioms, which may be confusing because the meaning of the whole group of words taken together has little, often nothing, to do with the meanings of the words taken one by one. To know this "hidden" meaning, it is necessary to listen to it and also to use it as many times as possible.

Here are some popular ones with their meanings and examples (There are others in the annex):

- **All ears** – Eager to listen; curious.
    - The secretary is all ears to what her boss has to say.

- **Apple of your eye** – A person or thing that is greatly loved, treasured.
    - The company is the apple of the president's eye.

- **Bite your tongue** – Take back or be ashamed of what you have said; struggle not to say something you want to say.
    - She had to bite her tongue in order not to give out the information about the new merger.

- **Break the ice** – To overcome the first awkward difficulties in a social situation by a friendly gesture.
    - He always tells a joke at the meetings to break the ice.

- **Call it a day** – to stop work for the day.
    - Let's call it a day after this long and tiring meeting.

Exercise Approaching Collocations

4. Complete the sentences with the words below:

speech   ice   people   language   contact
payment   message   business   policy   care

a) During the meetings, the manager always tells a joke to break the _____.
b) At the convention there was a crowd of _____ waiting to listen to the guest speaker.
c) During an interview, it's very important to keep eye _____.
d) People should be well-prepared to give a _____.
e) Characteristics of people's personality may be revealed by their body _____.
f) It's a pleasure to do _____ with your company.
g) The financial department sent us an e-mail because they hadn't received any _____ yet.
h) According to the company _____ it is forbidden to smoke in the premises.
i) The marketing department takes _____ of all the publicity seen on TV.
j) In case you have already made the payment, please disregard this _____.

Síntese do capítulo

Neste último capítulo, analisamos como escrever uma carta empresarial de maneira objetiva e cordial. Apresentamos também *phrasal verbs* e algumas dificuldades especiais relacionadas a esse assunto e propusemos exercícios de fixação. Abordamos, ainda, o discurso, uma ferramenta importante para o profissional da área empresarial. Por fim, investigamos algumas expressões idiomáticas, que, apesar de existirem em todas as línguas, são geralmente de difícil compreensão para estrangeiros.

considerações finais

Neste livro, abordamos o inglês instrumental, tendo sempre como foco o ambiente profissional empresarial. Nossa intenção, contudo, foi apresentar também aos leitores estratégias que os ajudassem na compreensão dos diversos gêneros textuais aqui explorados.

Para tanto, em cada capítulo, tivemos como preocupação dois pontos distintos: apresentar gêneros textuais diferentes e selecionar vocábulos significativos, relacionados à área empresarial. Visando à melhor compreensão dos textos analisados, enfocamos, ainda, tópicos gramaticais pertinentes em cada caso.

O domínio de uma língua estrangeira não é uma tarefa simples, pois depende de várias habilidades linguísticas. Acreditamos que, ao concluírem o estudo dos 12 capítulos que compõem este livro, nossos alunos estarão, certamente, bem mais perto de alcançar nosso objetivo, que é a compreensão de textos escritos em inglês, ou seja, a comunicação entre o escritor e o leitor de produções textuais em língua inglesa.

Desse modo, esperamos que este material seja de valia tanto para professores quanto para alunos.

Capítulo 1

1. *to guess* – adivinhar, adivinhação
2. *which* – que, o(s) qual(is), a(s) qual(is)
3. *to become* – tornar-se
4. *thinking* – pensamento
5. *to learn* – aprender
6. *readers* – leitores
7. *to increase* – aumentar
8. *understanding* – compreensão
9. *to make* – fazer
10. *knowledge* – conhecimento
11. *to remind* – lembrar
12. *to try* – tentar
13. *when* – quando
14. *gaps* – lacunas
15. *to find* – encontrar
16. *to mean* – significar
17. *to go back* – voltar
18. *instead* – em vez de
19. *failure* – fracasso
20. *employee* – empregado/a
21. *to provide* – fornecer
22. *support* – apoio
23. *to gather* – juntar
24. *assignments* – tarefas
25. *to supply* – fornecer
26. *to get up* – levantar da cama
27. *to take a shower* – tomar banho
28. *to get dressed* – vestir-se
29. *to have breakfast* – tomar café da manhã
30. *near* – perto
31. *far* – longe
32. *to ask* – perguntar
33. *to answer* – responder
34. *to write* – escrever
35. *to report* – relatório

Capítulo 2

1. *to manage* – gerenciar
2. *rather* – em vez de
3. *busily* – ocupadamente
4. *to book* – reservar
5. *headquarter* – matriz
6. *branch* – filial
7. *supply* – suprimento

8. *shift work* – rotina de trabalho com horários diferentes
9. *weather* – tempo
10. *to fall* – cair
11. *appointment* – compromisso
12. *step* – passo
13. *nowadays* – atualmente
14. *available* – disponível
15. *due to* – devido a
16. *skills* – habilidades
17. *to find out* – descobrir
18. *feelings* – sentimentos
19. *to fit* – encaixar, servir
20. *to become up-to-date* – atualizar-se
21. *to head* – encaminhar-se
22. *to look for* – procurar
23. *commited* – comprometido
24. *income* – renda
25. *to set aside* – separar
26. *employer* – empregador
27. *to improve* – melhorar
28. *to be willing* – estar disposto
29. *growth* – crescimento
30. *feature* – característica
31. *season* – estação

Capítulo 3

1. *deadline* – último dia de prazo para alguma coisa
2. *bullying* – intimidação por meio de maus-tratos
3. *duty* – dever
4. *harassment* – assédio
5. *support* – apoio
6. *environment* – meio ambiente
7. *to feel like* – sentir vontade
8. *to look forward to* – esperar ansiosamente
9. *to require* – solicitar
10. *to apologize* – desculpar-se
11. *attachment* – anexo

Capítulo 4

1. *to build* – construir
2. *within* – dentro
3. *sprawling* – estendida
4. *handicapped* – deficiente
5. *reliance* – dependência
6. *resilient* – resistente

7. *feasible* – viável
8. *sights* – pontos turísticos
9. *to delay* – atrasar
10. *to last* – durar
11. *floor* – andar/piso
12. *furniture* – móveis
13. *weather* – clima, tempo
14. *advice* – conselho
15. *baggage, luggage* – bagagem, malas
16. *to lend* – emprestar
17. *duties* – obrigações
18. *in touch* – em contato
19. *to ban* – proibir
20. *to be aware* – estar ciente
21. *reliable* – confiável

Capítulo 5

1. *to range* – variar
2. *casual clothes* – roupas do dia a dia
3. *suit* – terno, conjunto de duas peças, *tailleur*
4. *as soon as* – assim que
5. *however* – entretanto
6. *sign* – sinal, signo
7. *grudging* – rancoroso
8. *sensitive* – sensível
9. *sympathetic* – solidário
10. *weak-willled* – sem força de vontade
11. *inquisitive* – curioso
12. *faithful* – fiel
13. *straightforward* – simples, direto
14. *lucky* – sortudo
15. *healthy* – saudável

Capítulo 6

1. *seasonal* – da estação
2. *bowl* – tijela
3. *toast* – torrada
4. *bagel* – pequeno pão redondo com um furo no meio
5. *whole wheat bread* – pão de centeio
6. *muffin* – pequeno pão doce com frutas
7. *jam* – geleia
8. *lettuce* – alface
9. *shrimp* – camarão
10. *tuna* – atum
11. *scallions* – cebolinha verde

12. *cabbage* – repolho
13. *mushroom* – cogumelo
14. *eggplant* – berinjela
15. *steamed* – cozido a vapor
16. *clams* – mariscos
17. *broiled* – grelhado
18. *soft drink* – refrigerante
19. *breakfast* – café da manhã
20. *lunch* – almoço
21. *dinner* – jantar
22. *fork* – garfo
23. *knife* – faca
24. *spoon* – colher
25. *cutlery* – talheres
26. *farthest* – mais longe
27. *both* – ambos
28. *edge* – ponta
29. *to slurp* – beber ruidosamente
30. *napkins* – guardanapos
31. *to unfold* – desdobrar
32. *to tuck* – inserir
33. *shirt* – camisa
34. *red wine* – vinho tinto
35. *white wine* – vinho branco
36. *spitting out* – cuspir
37. *to swallow* – engolir
38. *to torn* – quebrar
39. *bite sized piece* – pedaço pequeno para comer
40. *butter* – manteiga

Capítulo 7

1. *loads of* – muitos(as)
2. *to share* – dividir, compartilhar
3. *personal belongings* – pertences pessoais
4. *concerned* – preocupado
5. *to answer the phone* – atender ao telefone
6. *tips* – sugestões
7. *helpful* – prestativo
8. *features* – características
9. *on hold* – em espera
10. *caller* – aquele que telefona
11. *to mind* – importar
12. *to call back* – ligar de volta
13. *to ride a motorcycle* – andar de motocicleta
14. *to ring* – tocar
15. *to teach* – ensinar

Capítulo 8

1. *to precede* – preceder
2. *attire* – roupas, vestimenta
3. *wise* – sensato
4. *to bind* – comprometer-se
5. *whilst* – enquanto
6. *aisle* – corredor
7. *customs* – alfândega
8. *TB (tuberculosis)* – tuberculose
9. *DTP (Diphtheria, Pertussis (whooping cough) and Tetanus)* – difteria, cocheluche e tétano
10. *to gather* – juntar
11. *to lift* – levantar algo

Capítulo 9

1. *due to* – previsto; devido a; por causa de
2. *to request* – requisitar
3. *early check-in* – registrar-se no hotel mais cedo que o horário normal
4. *late check-out* – pagar a conta e deixar o hotel mais tarde que o normal
5. *departure* – partida
6. *available* – disponível
7. *to take into account* – considerer
8. *that is, that is to say, I mean, in other words* – isto é, ou seja, em outras palavras
9. *to whom it may concern* – a quem possa interessar
10. *to arrest* – prender
11. *thief* – ladrão
12. *sharp knife* – faca afiada
13. *cottage* – casa de campo
14. *to hire* – contratar
15. *wisely* – sabiamente
16. *time to spare* – tempo para desperdiçar
17. *to miss a meeting* – perder um encontro
18. *loads of* – muito(a), muitos(as)
19. *to throw the garbage away* – jogar o lixo fora
20. *co-worker* – colega de trabalho

Capítulo 10

1. *entity* – entidade
2. *chair* – presidente, diretor
3. *outline* – resumo
4. *motions* – petições
5. *to proofread* – revisar
6. *to incur* – incorrer

7. *pool together* – associar interesses
8. *lecture* – palestra

Capítulo 11

1. *to make your interviewer's jaw drop* – fazer seu entrevistador ficar admirado, boquiaberto
2. *accomplishments* – realizações
3. *to imply* – sugerir, inferir
4. *confident* – confiante
5. *to breathe* – respirar
6. *small talk* – conversas irrelevantes
7. *further* – adicional
8. *storm* – tempestade
9. *cover letter* – carta de apresentação
10. *concerning* – no que diz respeito
11. *rough paper* – rascunho
12. *notice of dismissal* – aviso de demissão
13. *to assign* – designar
14. *to injure* – ferir
15. *to arrest* – prender
16. *to sack (to fire)* – despedir

Capítulo 12

1. *furthermore* – além do mais
2. *underneath* – abaixo de
3. *to puzzle* – refletir
4. *speech* – discurso, palestra
5. *foundation* – base
6. *to grasp* – entender
7. *to struggle* – esforçar-se, batalhar
8. *awkward* – constrangedor, inoportuno
9. *to annoy* – irritar, incomodar
10. *humbly* – humildemente
11. *hearty* – caloroso
12. *to hang* – pendurar, enforcar
13. *noose* – corda da forca
14. *to kick* – chutar
15. *to knock* – bater, socar
16. *sneaky* – sorrateiro, furtivo
17. *petty* – insignificante

Referências

ALBERTO ALVARÃES. Disponível em: <http://www.albertoalvaraes.adm.br>. Acesso em: 11 set. 2012.

BASIL RESTAURANT. Disponível em: <http://www.basilsminneapolis.com>. Acesso em: 10 mar. 2012.

BRITISH COUNCIL. **Using LearnEnglish Kids with Your Child**: Seasons. Disponível em: <http://www.britishcouncil.org/parents-tips-seasons.htm>. Acesso em: 11 set. 2012.

CAMBRIDGE DICTIONARIES ONLINE. Disponível em: <http://dictionary.cambridge.org/dictionary/british/lingua-franca>. Acesso em: 10 mar. 2012.

COLEMAN, H. The Top Ten Etiquette Tips For The Business Dinner or Interview. **Own The Dollar**. Disponível em: <http://ownthedollar.com/2009/05/top-ten-etiquette-tips-business-dinner-interview>. Acesso em: 9 mar. 2012.

CUESTA COLLEGE. **Understanding the Reading Process**. Disponível em: <http://academic.cuesta.edu/acasupp/AS/302.HTM>. Acesso em: 2 mar. 2012.

ECONOMICS NETWORK. **The Handbook for Economics Lecturers**. Cap. 3. Disponível em: <www.economicsnetwork.ac.uk/handbook/international/3>. Acesso em: 10 mar. 2012.

EHOW. **How to Present Yourself During a Job Interview**. 3 Oct. 2011. Disponível em: <http://www.ehow.com/how_2080218_present-yourself-during-job-interview.html#ixzz1oqN3ZVmn>. Acesso em: 10 mar. 2012.

GORMAN, T. The Top Advantages of Video Conferencing. **Ezine @rticles**, 26 Aug. 2006. Disponível em: <http://ezinearticles.com/?The-Top-Advantages-Of-Video-Conferencing&id=282728>. Acesso em: 10 mar. 2012.

HEATHFIELD, S. M. Work Dress Codes and Image Collection. **About.com**. Disponível em: <http://humanresources.about.com/od/workrelationships/tp/dress_code_collect.htm>. Acesso em: 9 mar. 2012.

MACFADYEN, H. What is a Conjunction? **uOttawa**, 2012. Disponível em: <http://www.writingcentre.uottawa.ca/hypergrammar/conjunct.html>. Acesso em: 15 out. 2012.

MERCURY, F. I Was Born to Love You. Intérprete: Queen. In: QUEEN. **Mr. Bad Guy**. New York: Columbia Records, 1984. Lado 1. Faixa 3.

MIND TOOLS. **How Good is Your Time Management?** Disponível em: <http://www.mindtools.com/pages/article/newHTE_88.htm>. Acesso em: 10 mar. 2012.

MORACHE, R. **Urban Transportation Choices**. 2005. Material não publicado.

O'NEILL, R. **Travel Wisely, Travel Well**. 22 Oct. 2005.

PHONE SENSE. **Answering the Phone Well**. Disponível em: <http://phonesense.blogspot.com/2006_04_01_archive.html>. Acesso em: 10 mar. 2012.

PROCTER, P. **Cambridge International Dictionary of English**. Cambridge: Cambridge University Press, 1995.

PROFESSIONAL SECRETARIAL SERVICES. **The Trip Adviser**: an Essential Tool for Organizing (Business) Travel. Disponível em: <http://www.professional-secretarial-services.com/trip-adviser.html>. Acesso em: 10 mar. 2012.

QOWL – Quality of Working Life. **Improving Quality of Working Life**. Portsmouth: Cardiff University, 2008. Disponível em: <http://www.cardiff.ac.uk/humrs/pwe/quality/0310%20Portsmouth%20Survey%20Results.doc>. Acesso em: 1º mar. 2012.

RIGG, S. How to Dress to Impress on Casual Friday. **eHow.com**. Disponível em: <http://www.ehow.com/how_5075097_dress-impress-casual-friday.html#ixzz1opncQoAt>. Acesso em: 9 mar. 2012.

ROSELAND, D. **Organizing a Business Trip**: A Technology-Integrated Project. Disponível em: <http://www.southasiaoutreach.wisc.edu/high%20school/businessTrip.htm>. Acesso em: 10 mar. 2012.

SMITH, D. H. **Sources of Negociation**. Disponível em: <http://www.ita-intl.com/homework8/sources_for_negotiation.html>. Acesso em: 11 dez. 2011.

SPRINGSTEEN, B. Born in the USA. Intérprete: Bruce Springsteen. In: SPRINGSTEEN, B. **Born in the USA**. New York: Columbia Records, 1894. Faixa 1.

TFL – Transport for London. **Key Facts**. Disponível em: <http://www.tfl.gov.uk/corporate/modesoftransport/londonunderground/1608.aspx>. Acesso em: 29 nov. 2011.

UE – Using English. **Formal Letter Writing**: How to Write Formal Letters. Disponível em: <http://www.usingenglish.com/resources/letter-writing.php>. Acesso em: 10 mar. 2012.

UNILEARNING. **The Purpose of The Purpose of Reports**. Disponível em: <http://unilearning.uow.edu.au/report/index.html>. Acesso em: 10 mar. 2012a.

_____. **Good and Poor Examples of Executive Sumaries**. Disponível em: <http://unilearning.uow.edu.au/report/4bi1.html>. Acesso em: 11 set. 2012b.

WISEGEEK. **What is Video Conferencing?** Disponível em: <http://www.wisegeek.com/what-is-video-conferencing.htm>. Acesso em: 10 mar. 2012.

YAHOO! VOICES. **Give the Perfect Speech Using 8 Easy Steps**. Disponível em: <http://voices.yahoo.com/give-perfect-speechusing-8-easy-steps-1488381.html>. Acesso em: 10 mar. 2012.

Apêndice 1

Verbos irregulares

Base Form	Past Tense	Past Participle	Portuguese Translation
arise	arose	arisen	surgir, erguer-se
awake	awoke	awoken	despertar
be	was, were	been	ser, estar
bear	bore	borne	suportar, ser portador de
beat	beat	beaten	bater
become	became	become	tornar-se
befall	befell	befallen	acontecer
beget	begot	begotten, begot	procriar, gerar
begin	began	begun	começar
behold	beheld	beheld	contemplar
bend	bent	bent	curvar
bet	bet	bet	apostar
bid	bid	bid	oferecer, fazer uma oferta
bind	bound	bitten	morder
bleed	bled	bled	sangrar, ter hemorragia
blow	blew	blown	assoprar, explodir
break	broke	broken	quebrar
breed	bred	bred	procriar, reproduzir
bring	brought	brought	trazer
broadcast	broadcast	broadcast	irradiar, transmitir
build	built	built	construir
buy	bought	bought	comprar
cast	cast	cast	atirar, deitar
catch	caught	caught	pegar, capturar
choose	chose	chosen	escolher
cling	clung	clung	aderir, segurar-se

come	*came*	**come**	vir
cost	*cost*	**cost**	custar
creep	*crept*	**crept**	rastejar
cut	*cut*	**cut**	cortar
deal	*dealt*	**dealt**	negociar, tratar
dig	*dug*	**dug**	cavocar
do	*did*	**done**	fazer
draw	*drew*	**drawn**	tracionar, desenhar
drink	*drank*	**drunk**	beber
drive	*drove*	**driven**	dirigir, ir de carro
eat	*ate*	**eaten**	comer
fall	*fell*	**fallen**	cair
feed	*fed*	**fed**	alimentar
feel	*felt*	**felt**	sentir, sentir-se
fight	*fought*	**fought**	lutar
find	*found*	**found**	achar, encontrar
flee	*fled*	**fled**	fugir, escapar
fling	*flung*	**flung**	arremessar
fly	*flew*	**flown**	voar, pilotar
forbid	*forbade*	**forbidden**	proibir
forget	*forgot*	**forgot, forgotten**	esquecer
forgive	*forgave*	**forgiven**	perdoar
freeze	*froze*	**frozen**	congelar, paralisar
get	*got*	**gotten, got**	obter
give	*gave*	**given**	dar
go	*went*	**gone**	ir
grind	*ground*	**ground**	moer
grow	*grew*	**grown**	crescer, cultivar
have	*had*	**had**	ter, beber, comer
hear	*heard*	**heard**	ouvir
hide	*hid*	**hidden, hid**	esconder

hit	*hit*	**hit**	bater
hold	*held*	**held**	segurar
hurt	*hurt*	**hurt**	machucar
keep	*kept*	**kept**	guardar, manter
know	*knew*	**known**	saber, conhecer
lay	*laid*	**laid**	pôr (posição horizontal)
lead	*led*	**led**	liderar
leave	*left*	**left**	deixar, partir
lend	*lent*	**lent**	dar emprestado
let	*let*	**let**	deixar, alugar
lie	*lay*	**lain**	deitar
lose	*lost*	**lost**	perder, extraviar
make	*made*	**made**	fazer, fabricar
mean	*meant*	**meant**	significar, querer dizer
meet	*met*	**met**	encontrar, conhecer
overcome	*overcame*	**overcome**	superar
overtake	*overtook*	**overtaken**	alcançar, surpreender
pay	*paid*	**paid**	pagar
put	*put*	**put**	colocar
quit	*quit*	**quit**	abandonar
read	*read*	**read**	ler
ride	*rode*	**ridden**	andar
ring	*rang*	**rung**	tocar (campainha etc.)
rise	*rose*	**risen**	subir, erguer-se
run	*ran*	**run**	correr, concorrer, dirigir
saw	*sawed*	**sawn**	serrar
say	*said*	**said**	dizer
see	*saw*	**seen**	ver
seek	*sought*	**sought**	procurar obter, objetivar
sell	*sold*	**sold**	vender
send	*sent*	**sent**	mandar

set	*set*	**set**	marcar, ajustar
shake	*shook*	**shaken**	sacudir, tremer
shed	*shed*	**shed**	soltar, deixar cair
shine	*shone*	**shone**	brilhar, reluzir
shoot	*shot*	**shot**	atirar, alvejar
show	*showed*	**shown**	mostrar, exibir
shrink	*shrank*	**shrunk**	encolher, contrair
shut	*shut*	**shut**	fechar, cerrar
sing	*sang*	**sung**	cantar
sink	*sank*	**sunk**	afundar, submergir
sit	*sat*	**sat**	sentar
slay	*slew*	**slain**	matar, assassinar
sleep	*slept*	**slept**	dormir
slide	*slid*	**slid**	deslizar, escorregar
sling	*slung*	**slung**	atirar, arremessar
speak	*spoke*	**spoken**	falar
spend	*spent*	**spent**	gastar
spin	*spun*	**spun**	fiar, rodopiar
spit	*spit, spat*	**spit, spat**	cuspir
spread	*spread*	**spread**	espalhar
spring	*sprang*	**sprung**	fazer saltar
stand	*stood*	**stood**	parar de pé, aguentar
steal	*stole*	**stolen**	roubar
stick	*stuck*	**stuck**	cravar, fincar
sting	*stung*	**stung**	picar (inseto)
stink	*stank*	**stunk**	cheirar mal
strike	*struck*	**struck**	golpear, desferir
string	*strung*	**strung**	amarrar
strive	*strove*	**striven**	esforçar-se, lutar
swear	*swore*	**sworn**	jurar, dizer palavrão
sweep	*swept*	**swept**	varrer

swim	*swam*	**swum**	nadar
swing	*swung*	**swung**	balançar, alternar
take	*took*	**taken**	tomar, pegar
teach	*taught*	**taught**	ensinar, dar aula
tear	*tore*	**torn**	rasgar, despedaçar
tell	*told*	**told**	contar
think	*thought*	**thought**	pensar
throw	*threw*	**thrown**	atirar, arremessar
tread	*trod*	**trodden**	pisar, trilhar
undergo	*underwent*	**undergone**	submeter-se a, suportar
understand	*understood*	**understood**	entender
uphold	*upheld*	**upheld**	sustentar, apoiar
wear	*wore*	**worn**	vestir, usar, gastar
win	*won*	**won**	vencer, ganhar
wind	*wound*	**wound**	enrolar, rodar, dar corda
write	*wrote*	**written**	escrever, redigir

Apêndice 2

Falsos cognatos

INGLÊS – PORTUGUÊS	PORTUGUÊS – INGLÊS
Actually (adv) – na verdade, realmente	*Atualmente* – nowadays, at present
Adept (n) – perito em algo	*Adepto* – supporter, follower
Agenda (n) – pauta, planos	*Agenda* – appointment book; schedule
Amass (v) – acumular, juntar, amontoar	*Amassar* – crush, dent, wrinkle
Anticipate (v) – prever; aguardar, ficar na expectativa	*Antecipar* – to bring forward, to move forward
Application (n) – requerimento, formulário, solicitação	*Aplicação (financeira)* – investment
Appointment (n) – hora marcada, compromisso profissional, consulta, nomeação	*Apontamento* – note, tally
Argument (n) – discussão, briga	*Argumento* – reasoning, point, plot
Assist (v) – auxiliar, ajudar	*Assistir* – to take care of someone, to watch
Assume (v) – presumir, supor	*Assumir* – to take on, to admit
Attend (v) – assistir, participar de, comparecer	*Atender* – to serve; to tend; to help, to answer
Audience (n) – plateia, público	*Audiência* – court appearance; interview
Baton (n) – batuta (música), cacetete, bastão	*Batom* – lipstick
Beef (n) – carne de gado	*Bife* – steak
Cafeteria (n) – refeitório tipo universitário ou industrial	*Cafeteria* – coffee shop, snack bar
Camera (n) – máquina fotográfica	*Câmara* – tube (de pneu) chamber (grupo de pessoas), hall
Carton (n) – caixa de papelão, pacote de cigarros (200)	*Cartão* – card
Casualty (n) – baixa (morte fruto de acidente ou guerra), fatalidade, vítima	*Casualidade* – chance
Cigar (n) – charuto	*Cigarro* – cigarette

Collar (n) – gola, colarinho, coleira	*Colar* – necklace
College (n) – faculdade, ensino superior	*Colégio (ensino médio)* – high school
Commodity (n) – artigo, mercadoria, produto	*Comodidade* – comfort, convenience
Competition (n) – concorrência	*Competição* – contest
Comprehensive (adj) – abrangente, amplo	*Compreensivo* – understanding
Compromise (v) – entrar em acordo, fazer concessão, ceder	*Compromisso* – appointment; date, engagement, commitment
Contest (n) – competição, concurso	*Contexto* – context
Convenient (adj) – prático	*Conveniente* – appropriate
Costume (n) – fantasia (roupa)	*Costume* – custom, habit
Data (n) – dados (números, informações)	*Data* – date
Deception (n) – trapaça, fraude, engano	*Decepção* – disappointment, disillusionment
Defendant (n) – réu, acusado	*Defesa* – defense, vindication
Design (v, n) – projetar, criar, projetar; modelo, plano	*Designar* – to appoint, to assign
Editor (n) – redator	*Editor* – publisher
Educated (adj) – instruído, culto	*Educado* – well-mannered, polite
Emission (n) – descarga, emissão de gases	*Emissão* – issuing (of a document etc.), broadcast
Enroll (v) – inscrever-se, registrar-se, matricular-se	*Enrolar* – to roll up; to wrap up; to reel
Eventually (adv) – finalmente, por fim	*Eventualmente* – occasionally, possibly
Exciting (adj) – empolgante, emocionante	*Excitante* – thrilling
Exit (n, v) – saída, sair	*Êxito* – success
Expert (n) – especialista, perito	*Esperto* – smart, clever
Exquisite (adj.) – primoroso, refinado	*Esquisito* – strange, odd
Fabric (n) – tecido	*Fábrica* – plant, factory
Genial (adj) – simpático, cordial	*Genial* – brilliant, talented
Graduate program (n) – curso de pós-graduação	*Curso de graduação* – undergraduate program
Gratuity (n) – gratificação, gorjeta	*Gratuidade* – the quality of being free of charge

Grip (v) – agarrar firme, apertar com força	*Gripe* – cold, flu, influenza
Hazard (n, v) – perigo, risco, arriscar	*Azar* – bad luck, unlucky
Idiom (n) – expressão idiomática	*Idioma* – language
Income tax return (n) – declaração de imposto de renda	*Devolução de imposto de renda* – income tax refund
Ingenuity (n) – criatividade	*Ingenuidade* – naivety, simplicity
Injury (n) – ferimento, lesão	*Injúria* – insult, abuse
Inscription (n) – gravação em relevo, dedicatória	*Inscrição* – registration, enrollment
Intend (v) – pretender, ter intenção de, tencionar	*Entender* – understand
Intoxication (n) – embriaguez, efeito de drogas	*Intoxicação* – poisoning
Jar (n) – pote	*Jarra* – pitcher
Journal (n) – diário, revista especializada	*Jornal* – newspaper
Lamp (n) – luminária, abajur	*Lâmpada* – light bulb
Large (adj) – grande, espaçoso	*Largo* – wide
Lecture (n) – palestra, sermão	*Leitura* – reading
Legend (n) – lenda	*Legenda* – subtitle
Library (n) – biblioteca	*Livraria* – book shop
Location (n) – localização, local	*Locação* – rental, lease
Lunch (n) – almoço	*Lanche* – snack
Magazine (n) – revista	*Magazine* – department store
Mayor (n) – prefeito	*Maior* – bigger
Medicine (n) – remédio, medicamento	*Medicina* – medicine
Moisture (n) – umidade	*Mistura* – mix, mixture, blend
Motel (n) – hotel de beira de estrada	*Motel* – love motel
Notice (v) – notar, aperceber-se; aviso, reparar	*Notícia* – news
Novel (n) – romance	*Novela* – soap opera
Office (n) – escritório	*Oficial* – official
Parents (n) – pais	*Parentes* – relatives

Particular (adj) – específico, exato	*Particular* – personal, private
Pasta (n) – massa, macarrão	*Pasta* – paste; folder; briefcase
Policy (n) – política (diretrizes)	*Polícia* – police
Port (n) – porto	*Porta* – door
Prejudice (n) – preconceito	*Prejuízo* – damage, loss
Prescribe (v) – receitar	*Prescrever* – expire
Preservative (n) – conservante	*Preservativo* – condom
Pretend (v) – fingir, fazer de conta	*Pretender* – to intend, to plan
Private (adj) – particular	*Privado* – private
Procure (v) – conseguir, adquirir, assegurar	*Procurar* – to look for, to search
Propaganda (n) – divulgação de ideias/fatos com intuito de manipular	*Propaganda* – advertisement, commercial
Pull (v) – puxar	*Pular* – to jump
Push (v) – empurrar	*Puxar* – to pull
Range (v) – variar, cobrir, dispor	*Ranger* – to creak, to grind
Realize (v) – notar, perceber, dar-se conta, ter consciência de	*Realizar* – to achieve, to execute, to accomplish
Recipient (n) – recebedor, destinatário, receptor	*Recipiente* – container
Record (v, n) – gravar, registrar, disco, gravação	*Recordar* – to remember, to recall
Refrigerant (n) – refrescante, líquido para baixar temperaturas	*Refrigerante* – soft drink, soda, pop
Requirement (n) – requisito, exigência	*Requerimento* – request, petition
Resume (v) – retomar, recomeçar	*Resumir* – summarize
Résumé (n) – *curriculum vitae*, currículo	*Resumo* – summary
Retired (adj) – aposentado	*Retirado* – removed, secluded
Senior (n) – idoso	*Senhor* – gentleman, sir
Service (n) – atendimento	*Serviço* – job
Stranger (n) – desconhecido	*Estrangeiro* – foreigner
Stupid (adj) – burro, idiota	*Estúpido* – impolite, rude
Support (v) – apoiar, sustentar	*Suportar (tolerar)* – to tolerate, to bear

Tax (n) – imposto

Trainer (n) – preparador físico, adestrador

Turn (n, v) – vez, volta, curva; virar, girar

Taxa – rate; fee

Treinador – coach

Turno – shift; round

Apêndice 3

Idioms

1. *Cool as a cucumber* – very calm; not nervous or emotional. Example:
   The new employee is cool as a cucumber. Nothing upsets him.

2. *Down-to-earth* – practical, sensible, realistic. Example:
   The new management is down-to-earth, simplifying all the procedures.

3. *Eleventh hour* – at the latest possible time; just before the absolute deadline. Example:
   The company was able to come up with a new product at the eleventh hour.

4. *In a nutshell* – in very few words; briefly; clearly and to the point. Example:
   The seminar was very good. The lecturer was able to present his ideas in a nutshell.

5. *Jack-of-all-trades* – a person who can do many different kinds of work well. Example:
   The office-boy can do anything you ask him. He's our jack-of-all-trades.

6. *Light at the end of the tunnel* – a long-searched-for answer, goal or success. Imagine you have a hard, long task to do. Example:
   After the financial crisis, the president finally saw light at the end of the tunnel.

7. *Make ends meet* – to earn just enough to live within one's income. Example:
   The company is in a very difficult financial crisis. They are being able just to make ends meet.

8. *Monkey business* – silliness or fooling around; dishonest or illegal activities. It has two meanings. Example:
   The secretary found out that the foreign branch was doing monkey business with the financial reports.

9. *Nitty-gritty* – the specific heart of the matter; the practical details; the fundamental core of something. Example:
   The accountants were able to work out the nitty-gritty of the financial problem.

10. *Pass the buck* – to pass on or make another person accept responsibility or blame for something one does not want to accept for his or her own. Example:
    The new sales rep is always passing the buck. He never assumes his own mistakes.

11. *Piece of cake* – an especially easy and pleasant task. Example:
    The secretary likes to work with her new director; it's a piece of cake.

12. *Rat race* – a fierce, unending, stressful competition in business or society. Example:
    The rat race in the business world now-a-days is very competitive.

13. *Sleep on it* – to put off making a decision until at least the next day so that you can think about it overnight. Example:
    The director decided to wait a little longer about the new hirings. He's going to sleep on it for a while.

14. *Up against the wall* – in big trouble; in a difficult and desperate situation. Example:
    My friend's company is up against the wall. He may lose his job.

15. *With flying colors* – with ease and great success; in triumph. Example:
    The new management passed their training course with flying colors.

Apêndice 4

Phrasal verbs

1. *Account for* – explicar, dar uma razão.
2. *Agree with* – concordar, ter a mesma opinião de outro.
3. *Apply for* – fazer um pedido formal para emprego ou permissão.
4. *Call back* – retornar uma ligação telefônica.
5. *Call off* – cancelar algo.
6. *Come up against* – enfrentar algo ou ter oposição.
7. *Cut down on* – reduzir o número de pessoas ou tamanho de algo.
8. *Deal with* – resolver, cuidar de algum problema ou negócio.
9. *Figure out* – entender, encontrar a resposta.
10. *Hand in* – entregar um trabalho, relatório.
11. *Hang up* – encerrar uma ligação telefônica.
12. *Hold on* – esperar, especialmente em uma ligação telefônica.
13. *Join in* – participar de alguma reunião, grupo.
14. *Look forward to* – esperar ou antecipar algo com prazer.
15. *Note down* – fazer alguma anotação por escrito.
16. *Pay back* – reembolsar.
17. *Put off* – adiar, marcar uma outra data.
18. *Pick up* – apanhar uma pessoa em algum lugar.
19. *Rely on* – confiar, depender.
20. *Rule out* – eliminar.
21. *Set up* – iniciar um negócio.
22. *Shop around* – comparer preços.
23. *Take off* – decolar de avião.
24. *Think over* – considerer.
25. *Turn down* – recusar.

Capítulo 1

1. Todas as afirmativas apresentadas apontam para o modo como não se deve proceder diante de um texto.

2. c

3. (g) clarificação
   (f) comparação
   (i) compreensão
   (d) dificuldades
   (e) experiência
   (c) imagens
   (j) informação
   (b) processo
   (h) solução
   (a) estratégias

4. c

5. (c) ocasionalmente
   (e) raramente
   (k) quinzenalmente
   (h) quase nunca, raramente
   (g) repetidamente
   (a) geralmente
   (b) alguma vez
   (j) todo o dia
   (f) regularmente
   (i) duas vezes
   (d) uma vez
   (l) de vez em quando

6. a) No, it isn't. It's a notebook.
   b) No, I am not. I am Brazilian.
   c) No, we aren't. We are secretaries.
   d) No, he isn't. He is a manager.
   e) No, it isn't. It's an old computer.
   f) No, they aren't. They are co-workers.
   g) No, they aren't. They are the new managers.
   h) No, he isn't. He is the office boy.

7. a) Mary **is** (be) a bank manager. Every morning she **gets** (get) up at 6 a. m., **takes** (take) a shower, **gets** (get) dressed, **has** (have) breakfast and **goes** (go) to work at 7:15. She usually **arrives** (arrive) at the office at about 7:50 because she **starts** (start) working at 8:00 o'clock. Twice a week, she **has** (have) lunch with her friends at an Italian restaurant near the company. She **doesn't have** (have – neg.) lunch at home as she **lives** (live) a bit far from her job. Sometimes

185

she **doesn't work** (work – neg.) in the bank in the afternoon because she **has** (have) meetings with the clients outside the company. Due to the rush hour, she **doesn't go** (go – neg.) back home by bus, she often **returns** (return) home in the evening by subway.

b) I **am** (be) a very efficient secretary. Every morning I **get** (get) up at 6 a.m., **take** (take) a shower, **get** (get) dressed, **have** (have) breakfast and **go** (go) to work at 7:15. I usually **arrive** (arrive) at the office at about 7:50 because I **start** (start) working at 8:00 o'clock. Twice a week, I **have** (have) lunch with my friends at an Italian restaurant near the company I **don't have** (have – neg.) lunch at home as I **live** (live) a bit far from her job. Sometimes I **don't work** (work – neg.) in the office in the afternoon because I **have** (have) meetings with the clients outside the company. Due to the rush hour, I **don't go** (go – neg.) back home by bus, I often **return** (return) home in the evening by subway.

8. a) Do you use the computer every day?
   b) Do you send e-mails?
   c) Do you make appointments?
   d) Do you interview new employees?
   e) Do you write reports?

9. a) Yes, I do./No, I don't.
   b) Yes, I do./No, I don't.
   c) Yes I do./No I don't.
   d) Yes I do./No I don't.
   e) Yes I do./No, I don't.

10. (b) the computer
    (a) to meet you
    (e) an appointment
    (c) an e-mail
    (d) candidates
    (g) morning
    (h) staff
    (f) hour
    (j) bye
    (i) do you do?

Capítulo 2

1. a) No, she isn't.
   b) She has breakfast with Mr. Brown, the marketing manager.
   c) She needs to take the CD with the advertisement
   d) She usually calls the court secretary at 12 o'clock.
   e) No, she isn't.
   f) She has an appointment with the doctor.

g) No, she isn't.
h) She has a business dinner at the Majestic Restaurant.

2. a) My favorite day is ....
   b) December, January and February.
   c) Monday to Friday.
   d) Yes, we do./No, we don't.
   e) I celebrate my birthday in ....

3. **Miss Smith**: Good morning. It's Miss Smith speaking.
   Miss Brown: Good morning, this is Miss Brown. How **are you doing**?
   Miss Smith: Fine, thanks. And you?
   Miss Brown: Not bad, thanks.
   Miss Smith: Miss Brown, **is the Internet working** ok on your floor?
   Miss Brown: No, **it is not working** today. **We are having** problems with the connection. Why?
   Miss Smith: Well, the director needs the Internet to take part in a video conference and he can't wait for a long time to have it connected. I thought the problem could be only on my floor.
   Miss Brown: Sorry, but this problem is everywhere in the country today.
   Miss Smith: All right. Do you have an idea when the connection will be ok again?
   Miss Brown: **They aren't connecting** it until this afternoon, unfortunately.
   Miss Smith: All right. Thank you very much for your help. Bye.
   Miss Brown: Welcome and goodbye.

4. Verb to be + sujeito + verbo + ing?

5. Sujeito + verbo *to be* + not + verbo +ing.

6. b

7. c

8. c

9. a) **This** will help you understand your values, which is important in choosing a career.
   b) It is relevant to identify **these** preferences because it will help you to choose your profession.
   c) **This** may not be the one which pays you the best initial salary.

10. a) Wrong.
    Look! The sun is shining.
    b) Right.
    c) Wrong.
    Mr. Smith's secretary writes e-mails every morning.

Chave de respostas

187

d) Right.
e) Wrong.
— Where are you going?
— I am going shopping for supplies.

11. a) is typing
    b) have
    c) goes
    d) is landing
    e) read
    f) arrive
    g) is writing
    h) write
    i) spends
    j) saves

12. a) She is buying computer supplies now.
    b) They are going to the new branch now.
    c) He is eating fish and chips now.
    d) She is ordering chops now.
    e) They are living in England now.
    f) He is writing dramas now.
    g) They are drinking water now.
    h) He is assisting Paula now.
    i) She is listening to the radio now.
    j) They are playing cards now.

13. a) The secretaries study English every day.
    b) The employees are playing football now.
    c) The secretary is watching TV now.
    d) We wash hands before meals every day.
    e) The girls are working now.
    f) The teacher is speaking English now.

14. a) Spring, summer, fall and winter.
    b) No, they don't.
    c) No, we don't.
    d) My favorite season is ....
    e) No, they aren't.
    f) June, July and August.

15. a) **There are** four seasons in a year and they are usually based on the weather.
    b) Near the equator, **there is** a rainy and a dry season.
    c) In the United Kingdom **there are** four seasons but the winter is not so cold, and the summer is not so hot.

d) In the south of Norway, for example, **there are** 19 hours of daylight in the middle of summer, and only 5 hours in the middle of winter.

16. (c) range
    (g) a career
    (b) reason
    (a) weather
    (f) world
    (i) vacation
    (h) into account
    (d) force
    (j) an appointment, a meeting
    (e) a goal

Capítulo 3

1. b

2. b

3.

Verbo	Forma afirmativa	Forma interrogativa	Forma negativa
have	had	Did you have?	No, I didn't.
do	did	Did you do?	No, I didn't.
visit	visited	Did you visit?	No, I didn't.
go	went	Did you go?	No, I didn't.
love	loved	Did you love?	No, I didn't.
study	studied	Did you study?	No, I didn't.

4.

Verbo no infinitivo	Verbo no passado
write	Wrote
meet	Met
move	Moved
have	Had
stop	Stopped

5. a) his
   b) her
   c) my
   d) Their
   e) our
   f) your
   g) their
   h) its

6. a) His is big (or large).
   b) Hers is impatient.
   c) Theirs is comfortable.
   d) Yours is nice.
   e) Yes, yours is clear.

7. a) I was born in .... (local).
   b) I was born in .... (ano).
   c) Most babies are born cesarean.
   d) I was .... (local).
   e) I was with my ....

8. b

9. a) (x) an early reply
      (x) seeing someone
      (x) going abroad
   b) (x) the phone
   c) (x) workaholic
      (x) bossy
      (x) demanding
      (x) hard-working
   d) (x) casually

Capítulo 4

1. a) I would prefer an ....
   b) Urban quality of life is handicapped by reliance on the automobile.
   c) My means of transportation to go to and from school/work is ....

2. a) It appeared on stations in 1908.
   b) It is 402 Kms.
   c) I am .... years old.
   d) It is 27.8 km far.
   e) It is 60 m high.
   f) I'm .... m tall.
   g) It's very (or not very) big.
   h) I take vacation ....
   i) 1,065 million passanger do it.
   j) It costs 4 pounds.
   k) I can finish it in ....

3. a) How long
   b) How much
   c) How often
   d) How high
   e) How far

f) How many
g) How much
h) How tall
i) How long
j) How old
k) How big

4. a) some wood
   b) some money
   c) some advice
   d) is the news
   e) noise
   f) some writing paper
   g) luggage
   h) furniture
   i) bread
   j) experience

5. a) itself – transportation
   b) themselves – people
   c) himself – person
   d) itself – rail system

6. a) What
   b) How much
   c) Where
   d) How long
   e) How many
   f) How often
   g) When
   h) How far
   i) Why

7. b

8. a) herself
   b) themselves
   c) myself
   d) ourselves
   e) yourself

9. a) reservation
   b) hire
   c) rent
   d) on vacation
   e) system
   f) single or a return
   g) trip
   h) rush

i) speed
j) stuck

Capítulo 5

1.

Noun	Verb	Adjective	Adverb
collection	to collect	X	X
employee	to employ	employed/unemployed	X
guidance	to guide	X	X
business	X	busy/unbusy	busily/unbusily
formality	X	formal/informal	formally/informally
interaction	to interact	X	X
normality	X	normal/abnormal	normally/abnormally

2. c

3. a) **A**: Who will win the next World Cup?
   B: I don't know. Maybe Brasil.
   A: I hope so.
   b) **A**: Who will the next president be?
   B: I don't know. Maybe…
   A: I hope so.
   c) **A**: What will next year's fashions be like?
   B: I don't know. Maybe the colour in fashion will be yellow.
   A: I hope so.
   d) **A**: Where will you be in ten years time?
   B: I don't know. Maybe in England.
   C: I hope so.

4. a) As soon as he arrives I will phone you.
   b) As soon as we decide about the job we will let you know.
   c) When you see Malcom, you won't recognise him.
   d) As soon as I pass my driving test I will buy a car.

5. Respostas pessoais. Exemplos:
   a) On the weekend, we are going to go for a walk in the park.
   b) They are going to visit their parents next month.
   c) He is going to watch the new program on TV.

6. (j) inferior
   (e) uninformed
   (f) ineffectively
   (g) unprepared
   (b) worse
   (h) badly-informed
   (i) unfair
   (a) younger, newer

(c) easy
(d) more

7. a) Today is colder than yesterday.
   Today isn't as hot as yesterday.
   b) Finance is less interesting than marketing.
   Finance isn't as interesting as marketing.
   c) Paul's salary is lower than Peter's salary.
   Paul's salary isn't as high as Peter's salary.
   d) Dutch is less useful than English.
   Dutch isn't as useful as English.
   e) Paul earns more than Peter.
   Peter doesn't earn as much as Paul.
   f) His French isn't as good as his Spanish.
   His French is worse than his Spanish.
   g) My office is larger than Jane's office.
   Jane's office is smaller than my office.

8. a) the most efficient
   b) the oldest
   c) the biggest
   d) the most profitable
   e) the best
   f) the worst

9. (e) casual or smart clothes
   (d) away
   (c) luck
   (b) seller
   (g) heels
   (a) deal
   (f) dressed

Capítulo 6

1. a) can't
   b) must
   c) could
   d) might
   e) may not
   f) can't
   g) must
   h) might
   i) can't

2. a) at
   b) on
   c) through

d) over
   e) from… to…
   f) around
   g) down
   h) up
   i) near
   j) at

3. (a) strong possibility (pode)
   (e) necessity (precisa)
   (c) some possibility (pode)
   (b, d, f) advice (deve)

4. c

5. a) (**I**) She cans drive a car.
   She can drive a car.
   b) (**I**) Can you to type?
   Can you type?
   c) (**I**) You don't must open that door.
   You must not (mustn't) open that door.
   d) (**C**) Must you go?
   e) (**I**) Last year I must work on Saturdays.
   Last year I had to work on Saturdays.
   f) (**C**) When do you have to leave?
   g) (**I**) We mustn't pay now, but we can if we want to.
   We don't need to pay now, but we can if we want to.
   h) (**I**) Would you like coming out with us?
   Would you like to come with us?
   i) (**C**) I should tell you everything.

6. a) on
   b) for
   c) in front of
   d) across/into
   e) by
   f) up
   g) in
   h) at
   i) in
   j) between

7. a) There is a notice outside the company saying: You mustn't step **on the grass**.
   b) I like to do my **job** early in the morning, before the other employees arrive at the company.
   c) She is a good assistant, but she can't deal with **the computer** very well.

d) On Friday evening, there is always a terrible traffic **jam** in the motorway.

e) I was late for work because we ran out of light and I **got stuck** in the lift.

f) When I go to a restaurant I usually have meat as the **main course.**

g) Where do you usually **have lunch** at noon? At home or at work?

h) What is the **speed limit** in Germany?

i) When I travel abroad, I prefer to have the **continental breakfast.**

j) My boss likes to have a look at the **vegetarian menu**, as he doesn't eat meat.

Capítulo 7

1.

Present Perfect affirmative	Present Perfect interrogative	Present Perfect negative
I have always been patient.	Have you moved and fixed your offfice yet?	I haven't finished it yet.
I have just filled all the customer's folders in the new cabinet.	Where have you put the printer?	I haven't moved.
I have just connected the printer.	Have you already moved to a more modern office?	X

2. a) George has worked in the lab since 9 o'clock.

   b) George and Anne have been partners for 53 years.

   c) I have learned English since 2009.

   d) I have worked in this company for 22 years.

   e) George has become the company's CEO since 2002. / George has become the company's CEO for 10 years.

3. a) since
   b) for
   c) for
   d) for
   e) for

4. (e) a linha está ocupada
   (d) passar a ligação
   (a) Kate Jones na linha
   (b) anotar um recado
   (c) aguardar na linha
   (f) desligar o telefone

5. (f) It is 8:00 a.m.
   (e) It is 8:00 p.m.
   (h) The staff are still waiting for the business trainer.
   (g) The staff waited for the business trainer for some time and the training class is now over.

(a) There are good job offers in the newspaper this week.
(b) There were good job offers in the paper last week.
(d) She lived in the USA from 1995 to 2005.
(c) She still lives in the USA.

6. a) Bill has worked in New York since 1990.
   b) I have worked as an engineer for a long time.
   c) The have already attended the training program.
   d) I have never met Mr. Watson before.
   e) She hasn't posted the Christmas cards to the customers yet.
   f) That is the longest letter I have ever written to a company.
   g) Have you ever been to Madrid on business?
   h) Tom has always wanted to be a famous lawyer.
   i) The sales staff have eaten in that restaurant many times.
   j) Mr. Smith has been to the USA on business for three times.

7. a) get through
   b) sales staff
   c) hard tasks
   d) taking messages
   e) hold the line
   f) hang up
   g) customers folders
   h) customers' accounts
   i) don't worry
   j) what a relief

Capítulo 8

1. a) walk
   b) learn
   c) be
   d) being
   e) working
   f) meet
   g) follow
   h) go
   i) drive
   j) staying

2. a) P
   b) H
   c) P
   d) H
   e) H
   f) P
   g) H
   h) P

i) H
j) H

3.
a) so
b) such
c) such
d) so
e) such

4.
a) enough
b) enough
c) too
d) enough
e) too

5.
a) used to work
b) used to give
c) used to work
d) used to be
e) used to surfing
f) used to staying
g) used to talking
h) used to watching
i) used to reading
j) used to have

6.
a) too
b) enough
c) enough
d) too
e) so
f) such
g) such
h) so
i) too
j) so
k) enough
l) such

7.
(a) business trip
(b) foreign country
(c) various presentations
(d) exchange rate
(e) cash advance
(f) make appointments
(g) booking flights and hotels
(h) local time
(i) goods to declare
(j) business traditions

Capítulo 9

1. b

2. **Pattern A:**
   a) The journalist who writes those interesting reports is a friend of hers.
   b) The fashion designer who designed the last fashion show is a cousin of ours.
   c) The professor who gives the computer science course is a colleague of theirs.

   Pattern B:
   a) The report which they read is quite interesting.
   b) The computer which they bought is very fast.
   c) The lecture that they attended was rather boring.

   Pattern C:
   a) Mrs. Brown, whose husband is the general manager, doesn't like to be on the spotlight.
   b) Mr. Green, whose employees are very loyal, doesn't like to expand business.
   c) Mrs. Gray, whose secretary is very efficient, doesn't like to work on Saturdays.

3. a) which/that
   b) whom
   c) which
   d) who
   e) who/whom
   f) who
   g) who
   h) whose
   i) whom
   j) whose

4. a) The man who is watering the plants is a gardener.
   b) The girl whose father is my assistant is a brilliant student.
   c) The woman who he hired yesterday will start tomorrow.
   d) My young sister, who you met at my office last week, has just graduated.
   e) My boss, who I have worked for 2 months, is not very kind to me.
   f) What is the name of the director who came here last night?
   g) Swimming, which is a good sport, makes people strong.

5. a) missed
   b) misunderstood
   c) summer clothes

6. a) **John**: No, when I arrived she'd just thrown it away.
   b) **John**: No, when I arrived she'd just read it.
   c) **John**: No, when I arrived she'd just gone away.

7. a) **John**: Yes, when I arrived, she hadn't thrown it away yet.
   b) **John**: Yes, when I arrived, she hadn't read it yet.
   c) **John**: Yes, when I arrived, she hadn't gone away yet.

8. a) Paul arrived late at work because he had missed the bus.
   b) George celebrated his victory with his co-workers because he had won the prize.
   c) A thief got into the company because they had left the door unlocked.
   d) He wasn't hired because he hadn't answered all the questions.

9. a) makes a reservation
   b) single bedroom
   c) early check-in
   d) late check-out
   e) due to arrive
   f) departure times
   g) time to spare
   h) as soon as possible
   i) facilities provided
   j) points to remember

Capítulo 10

1. a) A report is written to give a spoken or written account of something that has been observed, done, or investigated.
   b) Introduction; report an observation; quoting; speculating; generalizing; commenting; making a recommendation; summing up.
   c) I can write about a wide range of subjects.
   d) A report should be written in an accurate, objective and complete way, and it should have a clear purpose and a specific audience.

2. **Pattern A:**
   a) The car he drives is usually rented.
   b) The computer he uses is often hired.
   c) The houses he builds are always sold.
   d) The articles he writes are seldom published.

   Pattern B:
   e) The question wasn't understood.
   f) The witness wasn't believed.
   g) The letters weren't posted.
   h) The story wasn't remembered.

Pattern C:
i) The flight has already been authorized.
j) The repair has just been completed.
k) The money has always been deposited.
l) The cheque has never been cashed.

Pattern D:
m) The machine will be tested next month.
n) The product will be launched in March.
o) The cattle will be auctioned at Easter.
p) The paintings will be exhibited next week.

3. (c) ...has been disconnected.
   (a) ...will be sent to the winners.
   (e) ...should be received by e-mail.
   (b) ...were killed in the explosion.
   (g) ...is not permitted in the station.
   (d) ...had not been paid.
   (h) ...is currently being rebuilt.
   (f) ...was told to stay inside home

4) a) I lived in London until I left college.
   b) They'll be happy when this job is finished.
   c) He'd like to see you before you leave the office.
   d) Ann made coffee, while Bill toasted the bread.
   e) She speaks both Chinese and Japanese.

5. a) so
   b) before
   c) and
   d) although
   e) because
   f) and
   g) because
   h) and
   i) until
   j) although
   k) when

6. a) AV
   b) AV
   c) PV
   d) PV
   e) PV

7. a) A new contract was asked from the company by the customer.
   b) The job at the bank had already been offered to Mary, when we first met.

c) A notice of dismissal will be given to Mr. Jackson by the company.
d) Too many duties have been assigned to Mrs. Green by her employer.
e) The money is being lent to Mr. Smith by the bank.

8. (j) experts
   (a) account
   (i) sector
   (b) document
   (h) connection
   (c) purpose
   (g) conference
   (d) audience
   (f) technology
   (e) a recommendation

9. a) official document
   b) written account
   c) clear purpose
   d) communication technology
   e) make a recommendation
   f) outside experts
   g) business sector
   h) video conference
   i) Internet connection
   j) specific audience

Capítulo 11

1. a) Step 3
   b) Step 1
   c) Step 5
   d) Step 2
   e) Step 3
   f) Step 4
   g) Steps 3 and 5
   h) Step 1

2. a) I asked the assistant if he had done his work.
   b) His boss asked him if he had remembered to lock the drawer.
   c) The waiter asked the tour guide if they spoke Chinese.
   d) The manager asked the secretary if they had finished their tasks at work.

3. a) told/said
   b) asked/say
   c) said/spoke
   d) spoke/said

4. a) I told the driver I wanted to go to the airport.
   b) My father said there was a letter for me from the company I had sent my CV to.
   c) Everybody said it was a great company to work for.
   d) Sally said she was making a phone call.
   e) John asked Peter to close the door
   f) His mother told him to call his boss.
   g) She told her daughter about the big problem they were having with the new computers.
   h) Sue asked the sales team to give her a return on their sales.

5. a) John asked me if I was going home.
   b) Mary asked me if I had stayed for the lecture.
   c) My friend asked Peter if he lived there.
   d) I asked Joan if she had been there before.
   e) Susan asked her friend to stay a little longer.

6. a) apply for the post
   b) feel confident
   c) contact you by phone
   d) provide solutions
   e) prospective job
   f) keep to the point
   g) wear formal clothes
   h) be professional
   i) find information
   j) open doors

Capítulo 12

1. (g) to stop doing something
   (a) to cancel
   (i) to connect/disconnect something from electricity
   (b) to register at a hotel
   (f) to enter/leave a bus, car, train
   (h) to be something/somewhere in the end
   (c) to dispose of something
   (d) to complete a form
   (j) to dress
   (e) to discover

2. (c) give assistance
   (a) ignore
   (b) discuss something

3. a) dropped out
   b) black out
   c) make up

    d) ran away
    e) blow out
    f) set off
    g) check up
    h) kept/up
    i) sold out
    j) set up

4. a) ice
    b) people
    c) contact
    d) speech
    e) language
    f) business
    g) payment
    h) policy
    i) care
    j) message

Sobre as autoras

Thereza Cristina de Souza Lima

É especialista em Língua Inglesa, mestra e doutora em Estudos Linguísticos pela Universidade Estadual Paulista (Unesp). É ex-bolsista do Programa de Doutorado no País com Estágio no Exterior (PDEE), Universidade de Manchester, promovido pela Coordenação de Aperfeiçoamento de Pessoal de Nível Superior (Capes). É também membro do grupo de pesquisa Tradução, Terminologia e Corpora (cadastrado no Conselho Nacional de Desenvolvimento Científico e Tecnológico – CNPq) e do projeto de pesquisa Padrões de Estilo de Tradutores (PETra), coordenado pela Profª. Drª. Diva Cardoso de Camargo, ambos (grupo de pesquisa e projeto) desenvolvidos na Unesp. No presente, atua como professora de Língua Inglesa no curso de Secretariado, professora de Língua Portuguesa nos cursos de Contábeis e Segurança no Trabalho e professora de Linguística Textual no curso de Letras, todos no Centro Universitário Uninter. Além disso, é professora de Linguística de Corpus no curso de especialização em Língua Inglesa: Metodologia do Ensino e Tradução da Pontifícia Universidade Católica do Paraná (PUCPR). Com 30 anos de experiência na área de ensino de idiomas, já ministrou aulas de língua inglesa em várias instituições de ensino superior, entre as quais a Universidade Santa Úrsula (Rio de Janeiro) e as Faculdades Integradas Ruy Barbosa (São Paulo). Foi também professora de língua e literaturas de língua inglesa na Universidade Federal do Mato Grosso do Sul (UFMS).

Carmen Terezinha Koppe

É graduada em Letras Inglês/Português pela Universidade Tuiuti do Paraná (UTP) e também especialista em Língua Inglesa: Metodologia e Tradução pela Pontifícia Universidade Católica do Paraná (PUCPR) e em Ensino e Cultura de Línguas Estrangeiras, ênfase em Português para Estrangeiros, pela Universidade Federal do Paraná (UFPR). Atua como professora de língua inglesa desde 1990 e de língua portuguesa para estrangeiros desde 2004. Tem experiência nas seguintes instituições: Centro Cultural Brasil-Estados Unidos de Curitiba, Núcleo de Assessoria Pedagógica (NAP-UFPR), Curso de Secretariado da Faculdade Internacional de Curitiba (Facinter), Núcleo de Línguas da PUCPR, Centro Europeu, Cetep Ensino, Módulo Editora (como revisora de material didático de inglês). Além disso, é professora particular de inglês e tradutora autônoma de inglês-português-inglês. Participa do Regional Interest Group (RIG – Grupo de Estudo) de Tradução do Braz-Tesol Regional Chapter Curitiba. Viveu, estudou e trabalhou em Nova Iorque durante 24 anos.

Impressão: Serzegraf
Março/2014